The Taste For Things That Are True

Former journalist and photographer, Henri Tracol witnessed the Spanish Civil War as head of a Republican press agency. Later he worked at the Musée de l'Homme in Paris and also became a sculptor. For ten years he was a close pupil of G. I. Gurdjieff. He is one of the leading exponents of Gurdjieff's teaching and is currently President of the Gurdjieff Institute in France.

Henri Tracol

The Taste For Things That Are True

ESSAYS AND TALKS BY A PUPIL OF G. I. GURDJIEFF

Henri Tracol

ELEMENT

Shaftesbury, Dorset ● Rockport, Massachusetts
Brisbane, Queensland

© Henri Tracol 1994

First published in Great Britain in 1994 by
Element Books Limited
Shaftesbury, Dorset SP7 8BP

Published in the USA in 1994 by
Element Books, Inc.
42 Broadway, Rockport, MA 01966

Published in Australia in 1994 by
Element Books Limited for
Jacaranda Wiley Limited
33 Park Road, Milton, Brisbane 4064

Reprinted 1995

Cover design by Max Fairbrother
Designed by Gerald Larn
Typeset by Aldridge Print Group, London SW16
Printed and bound in Great Britain by
Redwood Books Limited, Trowbridge, Wiltshire

British Library Cataloguing in Publication
data available

Library of Congress Cataloging in Publication
data available

ISBN 1–85230–468–5

This selection of essays, talks and interviews forms part
of an anthology published in France in 1983 by Editions
Pragma under the title *Pourquoi dors-tu, Seigneur?* Some of
them first appeared in the USA in *Parabola*, a quarterly
magazine, devoted to the study of myth and meaning.

They all shed light, sometimes direct, sometimes
indirect on many aspects of Gurdjieff and his teaching.

Contents

Foreword

A handful of disparate texts, the oldest going back more than fifty years – what, then, is the purpose?

Let me say at once, I do not consider myself a writer, and this is not (the very slim) Volume I of my complete works. In any case one thing is certain: there will not be a Volume II.

More simply, several friends asked me, not without a certain insistence, to gather together some writing, articles and lectures, with a view to a *private* publication, reserved for those who know me, and their friends. And, in the end, I said "Yes".

As for choice – I had accumulated in my drawers files full of papers from the days when I was a globe-trotter, photographer and journalist by profession: some accounts of conversations in which I took part and private notebooks in which I noted my impressions of everything which seemed to me to answer a quest already felt as essential.

In a word, each time, through the years, that I immersed myself in these papers I came out of them perplexed to say the least and somewhat at sea, promising myself, in conclusion, to make a wild and vengeful bonfire of them. So, the little I have kept can be considered literally as saved from the flames.

"There is a heroism in acting without any other sanction than the intoxication of moving in the direction which is truly one's own."

These words of my uncle, Elie Faure,* have accompanied me unceasingly since adolescence. And from decade to decade they resound in me more and more like a call to free me, among other things, from the childish fascination with results, with 'progress' accumulated like a possession. It is by repeatedly divesting himself of his layers of clothing that a being comes to life.

It is in this spirit therefore that I have attempted to collect these sparse and scattered pages, beginning with the oldest ones.

From dreams and revolts we move to another stage, that of studies, questions on culture and then to the rediscovery of traditional perspectives.

* Eminent art historian but also a traveller and philosopher.

But all this only makes sense when related to what secretly animated it from 1938 onwards: my first contacts with Mme de Salzmann and the teaching of G.I. Gurdjieff. So I have kept for last the various testimonies to this which I have been called upon to make, sometimes abroad and sometimes in France.

Along the way I have appealed to Luc Dietrich.** Most cherished friend and companion, he took the trouble, towards the end of 1943, to address to each one of his closest friends a notebook of questions of a confidential nature. I have chosen from them the ones which, through my answers, evoke best the secret direction offered me since childhood.

** Author of *Dialogue de l'Amitié, Apprentissage de la Ville*, died 1944, aged 31.

Questions put to Henri Tracol by Luc Dietrich

L.D. – What differentiates your childhood most forcibly from your present state?

H.T. – I often want to weep for my defunct childhood, prolonged so tardily, however, that it survives to this day and shows through so many movements, thoughts, intonations – this phrase – to weep for – is proof of that. I mourn my impulses, my sensitivity, my enthusiasm and the clarity of my hope in God.

But what then have I lost, essentially? My trust, my confidence. I have ceased to believe so strongly in my lucky star. And yes, I have stopped waiting in all tranquillity to be helped, to be carried on someone's shoulders, to be protected, comforted, encouraged. And I have learned that before counting on a true, authentic, efficacious help it was necessary for me to deserve it, to work on myself without respite – and in silence.

What makes the difference, to-day, is the sense of gravity, of seriousness.

L.D. – What is your best childhood memory?

H.T. – Honestly I cannot answer . . . I always feel incredibly disarmed when I try to evoke my childhood. As soon as I try to hold on to them by their coat tails the slightest memories plunge into the mist and everything is confused, right up to the heart of adolescence. And when at last I think I have seized hold of one I have the impression it has gone through so many shifts it has lost all authenticity. And if there are any memories about which I have not the slightest doubt, I do not know what their real importance is . . . Perhaps my feelings in front of nature? The most distant memory is certainly this: I was about 3½ or 4 years old. I was alone at the bottom of the kitchen garden at Viarmes (the countryside of my childhood). It was evening, an hour before sunset. I had gone into a patch of wild barley or rye, and the ears of grain were swaying above my head, bathed in golden light. Standing still I tasted this bliss without end. I recall just that.

L.D. – What were your greatest joys as a child?

H.T. – My greatest *joys?* I will only speak of the ones I am sure about. After the departure of my mother it was, of course, every time I could see her again, even for an hour. During my childhood I had several "adorations": my great-aunt, my cousin, a half-sister of my mother's, etc . . . And I jumped for joy at the thought of seeing them again. Setting out on journeys and excursions. I have always had a profound joy on leaving the daily surroundings – don't forget, I am the nephew, the great-nephew and the great-grandson of geographers who travelled widely and undertook dangerous explorations . . . Other unforgettable moments too were when "tante Mignon" (a half-sister of my mother's) told us stories. How many fairy tales and Russian folk tales she told us and acted out for us unstintingly, her voice never betraying the slightest fatigue. And then, later – and for a period of two to three years – my greatest joys were of a religious kind. I ask to be baptised, then, each week, the Communion lifts me up above myself and opens me to states I would so much wish to taste again to-day – or their equivalent.

L.D. – What has been the influence of the cinema on your life?

H.T. – When I was 20 I was completely hypnotised by the cinema. I thought I had found my language there and I "thought cinema" all the time. I dreamed of films where certain visual revelations that I had would be able to express themselves naturally . . . That was at the time of "silent" films. The era of "the talkies" coincided with the opening of my cinema reviews in the magazine "Vu", which I kept up for four years. From then on, measuring better, as a particularly attentive and conscientious spectator, how much the sort of film I loved demands in effort, mastery, ability and maturity, I slowly got used to the idea of having a belated career – I would bring out my first film between the ages of 45 and 50, condensing in that work all the experience I would by then have acquired in life as well as in the studio corridors. And I recorded a good deal of my interest in the subject matter of films. I sought in my reviews to define the intimate meaning of the stories – what experiences they were recounting, what knowledge of a place, a period, a mentality, a collective or an individual drama, they were able to bring to us . . . But I had ceased to regard the screen as a more or less permissible pretext for visual juggling. I had, besides, the impression of enriching myself weekly with a portion of, a share in, existences lived through in a few hours, but with the intense desire to take part in them as intimately as possible in order to draw from them the maximum amount of substance.

L.D. – What, at the moment, is for you the greatest obstacle to the "work"? And how do you explain it?

H.T. – Absurdity of my efforts to-day: it is the work in the void of someone who has not yet dared to choose. But I am too cowardly, aren't I?, to rebel. An enormous resignation takes possession of me, engulfs my efforts, my questions – because, deep down, I am afraid, *afraid to know what I want*. That's it – my greatest obstacle: fear of choosing, which means, on the one hand: fear of giving up thousands of "possibilities". I discover all of a sudden how much I cling to these fancies, as soon as there is some question of getting rid of them.

Without desire the second before, I dream now recklessly of distant journeys. I cling desperately to projects for books, films, reviews, publishing, research centres or what have you. And, on the other hand, fear of coming a cropper in full ascent if I do decide to "take off" – and of falling again lower than on departure.

The Taste for Things That Are True

This essay was written when the author was in his twenties and at the beginning of his search, or, as he puts it in his book, "some thirty years before May 1968" – the date of the student uprisings in Paris.

We young ones were hungry. Our appetite was law; we absolutely had to taste everything, know everything, satiate ourselves with everything. We had read, reread, and catalogued all the most variegated and extravagant bills of fare. Our eyes shone at the mere sight of the appetizers; when the main dishes appeared, we shouted with enthusiasm.

Poor innocents. There are no words for what this banquet was – and still is. Under the sauces which were too clever to be honest, there was only spoiled meat, vegetables no longer fresh, fruit three-quarters rotten. The few morsels that were good were all mixed up with the worst. The more appetizing the plate looked, the less it contained. Everything smelled of adulteration, artifice, machine oil, and the chemical factory.

For this is the way it is: with our cooks, whether they are philosophers, politicians, industrialists, sportsmen, economists, writers, or artists, the aim is to imitate or to conceal *the taste of things that are true*. And so keen is our appetite at first that we devour everything eagerly. We lick the plates and ask for more. But soon enough weariness, the memory of imaginary feasts, and sluggish digestion have their effect. Tired of stuffing ourselves to no purpose, we beg (or demand) to be given at least some nourishment worthy of the name; and immediately our pseudo-master-cooks bestir themselves and bustle about arguing, only to wind up offering us (or forcing on us) some new concoctions. But, under other names, we are always seved the same dishes.

No words, indeed, for such a banquet. But I ask you, what then can we say about the guests? Because the worst of it is that in spite of everything we should still be sitting today at the same table with the same disgusting messes in front of us, and to crown it all, that we have wound up by acquiring a taste for them.

No doubt, such persistence is laughable; but all the same, it's a serious matter. For if we go on cheating our hunger, tomorrow we will kill it. All that will remain will be that artificial hunger, at once

Reprinted by kind permission of the late D. M. Dooling, founding editor of PARABOLA magazine where it appeared in Vol. IX, No. 1, 1984, on Hierarchy.

tyrannical and servile, that obeys instantly the smallest solicitation from without – and makes us its slaves.

Do you remember how we experienced with all our being the need to live fully? Life, naked life, was in front of us. We wanted to chuck into the fire all that cheap finery that decked out our purpose; sweep away the dubious company of half-truths, half-feelings, half-decisions; the crowd of walk-ons made up as scholars, poets, civilizing heroes, with their big empty words and their spectacular gestures; tear down finally all the cardboard stage sets in front of which they played out their comedy for us, but behind which, surely, *something* must be happening . . .

Remember how so many questions had us by the throat, which have gone unanswered. And since then, we've dared to make fun of them, we've dared to deny them, because it's the fashion to be skeptical, reasonable – that is, not to search *sincerely* any more to understand.

And yet – at the start, for us, to *understand* didn't mean to penetrate the skillfully arranged labyrinth of some philosophical theory; it didn't mean to accumulate thousands of fragments of information in order to fit them ingeniously together in the laboratory; on the contrary, it meant to seize reality with open arms, in the midst of life; and to look at it bravely, as the only way to become men.

I see you shrug your shoulders; I hear you snicker. But remember how it was: to understand, for us then, meant the opposite of words. We had to act, to risk our safety, our lives, make dangerous experiments; we had to measure ourselves in action, to know our possibilities and our limits not in the abstract but in the full exercise of our functions. We felt the need to play to the hilt our role among other people, so as to discover the meaning of our presence in the world. We felt the need to believe, to love, to commit ourselves, to march shoulder to shoulder towards a common ideal.

Do you remember? We had no words harsh enough, then, for the lukewarm, the sleepyheads, for sulking adolescents, for cowards and mollycoddles, for "philosophizers" in bedroom slippers and abstainers of every kind. For all those defeated before they began, all those who accepted to be bought off cheaply to lead a dog's life, we had only one cry: "Back to your kennels!"

But I ask you: what have we ourselves made of our enthusiasms? We have been traitors and perjurers; we in our turn have become deceivers, sleight-of-hand artists; we know all the ins and outs of performing conjurers' tricks with the only real, living questions. We have learned to be crafty with ourselves, to manipulate irony, to "philosophize," to dismiss, kindly, as "infantile," the manliness of our former search.

Already lethargy is creeping up on us. Already, at the least alarm, with our snail-like reflexes, we rush to reenter the deepest hollow in our mental shells. We take our stand in previously established positions; we refuse to expose ourselves.

What then has happened? Why have we deserted? From whence comes this progressive numbness, this sliding toward death of all that was most alive in us?

It came on by itself, stealthily, like a creeping infection – as the consequence of who knows what dangerous illusions or premature discouragement. From one disappointment to another, the sickness has taken a progressively deeper hold, gradually chasing us out of ourselves.

For that is where the trouble lies: what we didn't have courage enough to look for *inside*, we have thought we could find *outside*. Not that we have given up hope of a change, of a better use of our powers; but without knowing it, we have stopped really counting on ourselves to bring that about. Not that we have given up entirely, but now we wait for a miracle from outside. And we have begun to have wild dreams of favorable circumstances, of better conditions of life, or of some exceptional encounter. To feed our hopes, we have pounced greedily on the most absurd fictions and the stupidest arguments; we flung ourselves at the stockpile of ready-made notions, at the leftovers of the great thinkers, at the whole doctrinal flea market. Anything would do to save us from the terrible effort of facing ourselves.

We were afraid, of course, in front of life, and tried to escape. But the endless circle of the imagination is vicious indeed. Between the tyranny of our dreams and the bitterness of our awaking, we were wholly caught in the cogwheels. In the too-bright light of the sun, we preferred the shadows of our dreams, and then blamed the whole universe because they vanished.

So we began demanding everything from others; from society or from chance – and nothing from ourselves. Soon it was on these others, on society or misfortune, that we were heaping the blame for all our defeats.

We cry that we have been cheated, hoaxed, duped. But who began it? We have deserved these falsehoods a hundred times over. What am I saying? It was we who called them, adopted them, warmed them in our bosoms, fattened, pampered, and cherished them in order to flaunt them and carry them around in triumph. Who among us doesn't daily take his wishes for reality? If we fool ourselves like this, where will we find the strength to resist the lies that flatter our secret preferences?

"Whose fault is it?" That's our great cry. For every one of our failures, individual or collective, we must have at all costs someone to blame. At all costs we must find out who is responsible and chastise him thoroughly – sometimes one, sometimes another; there is always a scapegoat.

But our worst misfortune is just that: *no one is responsible* – ourselves less than anyone. We spend our time refusing all responsibility, even for our thoughts. We claim to have an answer for everything, but no longer wish to be answerable for anything.

In our frantic flight away from ourselves, we nevertheless feel a need for brotherhood, for walking side by side, which draws its strength from the same source as our deepest and truest emotions. But after the first professions of faith have been exchanged, why do we come together? To congratulate ourselves, to complain, to lull each other to sleep – or to make common property of all our hate and rancor. So in the group we are part of, we hurry to repeat the mistakes we already made with ourselves. It is always "the others" who are wrong; we, collectively, are excused. We consolidate our lies, we multiply them; and above all, we convince ourselves that we are strong. But the union of the worst weaknesses has never created strength.

When will we understand true brotherhood? If you are my brother, it's not flattery or sympathy I expect from you, but questions, provocations, a challenge; then you can help me, not before. If you are my brother, don't leave me in peace, don't let me go to sleep; my life is at stake. If we are brothers, we will rediscover together the hunger we knew when we were twenty, and the questions that had us by the throat – questions that have no answer except in the struggle for self-mastery and the conquest of our lives. Only that struggle can give us the taste for things that are true.

If we are sick to death of the sham banquet, who keeps us here? Let's leave this table of deceptions and go together in search of real food. Let us, too, return to earth – return to the abandoned field of our own lives, and clear, plow, fertilize, and cultivate this unworked ground that has been invaded by weeds. And when harvest time comes, we will go and tell our other comrades how bread tastes that one has kneaded with one's own hands.

L.D. – Before the "work", what idea restored your strength and confidence (in times of despair and discouragement?)

H.T. – I felt myself to be "in full formation" until very late and happy to be so. So many years ahead of me "to develop", to try everything, experience everything! A disorderly curiosity sustained me and, even more, a sort of poetic delirium in front of an ocean of possibilities. I gave free rein to my dreams which were as vast and assorted as they were nebulous and hazy. Despair and discouragement grabbed me by the throat every time my real abilities, my real means, hit me in the face: the discovery of my pathetic limits snatched me from my airy visions – not to make me face things, but to engulf me in the most sterile self-pity. Not for long, however: I came out of this state with childish plans for immediate or long-term revenge: it was my wish to live, "to live intensely" which swept me along again. But later, when I was overcome with anguish at all those wasted years, the thing which – for lack of immediate confidence – gave me the courage to go on was a certain feeling of fatality – I mean a "fatality" which would, in the end, be favourable to me. However obscure the ways of destiny might be, I had the secret conviction that there had always been hidden strengths lying within me and that I simply needed to have patience, to await with fervour their day of dawning. It was at the time when I had taken for myself (attributing to it a special meaning) the motto of the Duc d'Aumale: "I will wait."

The Mystery of Rebirth

This essay was translated and adapted by the late D. M. Dooling from "Homme, ciel, terre," which first appeared in L'Age Nouveau, No. 112. A talk with Henri Tracol follows the article.

"**A**t the momentof creation," says the Zohar, "the four cardinal points unite with the four constituent elements of the world here below: fire, water, earth, and air. It was by mixing these four elements that the Holy One, blessed be He, created a body in the image of that above. The body is thus composed of the elements of both worlds, those of the world below and those of the world above."

Two worlds: Heaven and Earth. And between these two worlds, there is a ladder, each rung representing an intermediary world, a level of realization, a degree of participation in the total Being. In the mysteries of Mithra, each corresponds to one of the seven planetary spheres that the initiate traverses, one after another, before attaining the highest Heaven. This is the ladder of Seth, whose posts were supported by the four sons of Horus to allow the dead Pharaoh to enter Heaven. It is the ladder of light which was to lead Mahomet from the ruins of the temple of Jerusalem to the foot of the divine Throne. It is Jacob's ladder, of which St. John was to say: "Henceforth ye shall see Heaven open, and the angels of God ascending and descending *upon the Son of Man.*"

But any attempt to push the analogy too far is bound to fail if too much weight is put on surface resemblances. The only way to avoid useless correlations, and to penetrate closer to the source of the common essence of traditional wisdom, is with a more open interest, a freer inner movement. This means putting oneself in a state of *resonance* to the vibration of the true analogy; this is the key to that universal symbolic language which we lost the use of so long ago. For even within a single tradition, there may be differing views; numbers and terms often disagree. Brahmanic thought holds to the division of the Tribhuvana: Heaven, Atmosphere, Earth. However, according to the Upanishads, the being who, after the death of his physical body, is reintegrated into the primordial unity by the *dêva-yâna*, passes first through the Kingdom of Fire, whose Ruler is Agni, then through the various domains of the Rulers of the day, that of the bright half of the

Published in PARABOLA magazine Vol. X, No. 3, 1985 on The Body and reprinted here by kind permission of the Editors.

lunar month, those of the months of the Sun's ascension, and finally that of the year.*

Israel, like Islam, distinguishes seven earths under the seven firmaments, some gloomy or arid, others fertile and drenched with light, peopled according to their level of being by the degenerate descendants of Adam and of Cain.

The Chinese, for their part, count nine heavens, but here again we find the idea of the Axis of the World – in the *Kien-Mou*, an erect piece of wood analogous to the sacrificial stake of the Brahman, or to the shaman's birch tree, cut into seven, nine, or sixteen notches – "by which the Sovereigns ascend and descend."

In the course of these ascensions the spiritual "space traveler" is often called upon to rid himself gradually of his various "garments," so that he can put on the "tunic of light" which becomes a sort of reflection of his own transformed being. The garments are the different "bodies," the temporary supports of an inner process of becoming.

But what misapprehensions we weave into these bodies! Since there is nothing within or outside of us that remains motionless, it is a little absurd to try to enclose the moving aspects of our being in summary concepts. Besides, the multiplicity of the systems proposed and their differences of opinion soon put a stop to this sort of self-limitation. The points of view are so different that there is no use in trying to establish an exact correspondence, for instance, between the four bodies of Christianity – the carnal, natural, spiritual, and divine – and the five envelopes (*koshas*) described by the Vedanta, in their relation with the three *shariras* – principial or causal form, subtle form, gross or corporeal form. It is the general movement that we need to understand, and the meaning of the relationships established between the elements of each doctrine as a whole.

On the other hand, this ascension has for an accompanying theme (though in an opposite sense) the "fall" of the soul into forms which are increasingly material and gross. The very idea of the liberation of the imprisoned soul by its escape from the accursed body plunges us directly into Manicheism – whereas man's true destiny on earth is linked to his effort to bring about the laborious fusion of the opposing tendencies in himself.

"One cannot move the soul without the body, nor the body without the soul," writes Plato,* and St. Thomas Aquinas speaks of a

* See René Guénon, *Man and His Becoming according to the Vedanta*.
* *Timaeus*.

"natural inclination" of the soul to unite with the body; "considered as the height of human perfection, the soul is not able to live separated from the body."**

For a human being also, the mystery of incarnation exists. How can he approach it? For it is not enough to awaken to the evidence of a more inner, more subtle presence. It is necessary to have an exchange in which he takes part as a whole being. He must acquaint his body and its members with what his head and his heart have welcomed.

It is at this point that Jacob's ladder is set up in him, with angels bearing messages ascending and descending. Between these two poles of his presence, between his Heaven and his Earth, a new life circulates, in which he is now beginning to believe.

"I am a doubting Thomas," say the sceptics. And the orthodox look at them scornfully – or rather, through them, at St. Thomas himself. Both would do well to take another look. Judas betrayed, Peter denied, Thomas doubted – how easy it is to say this!

Thomas – one of the twelve whom Christ himself chose and appointed and who remained close to him even after the "hard sayings" of Capernaum; who followed his Master everywhere, shared his trials, was present at his miracles. He was there when Jesus went into the house of Jairus, whose daughter had just died, and he took her by the hand and bade her rise; when the son of the widow of Nain sat up in his coffin and began to speak; he was there when Lazarus arose from his sepulchre at his Lord's command. He needed no conviction of Jesus' divinity. He believed in it, not with a sanctimonious and bigoted belief but with all the force of an inner certainty which was to lead him, in spite of taunts and threats, even to the Mount of Olives. After the "It is finished," he was still there, one of the eleven who remained united in their faith.

What did he still need to see? What new proof was necessary for this believer? What was the nature of the doubt that arose in him? He was an apostle. He had fully accepted his mission. He felt himself pledged, "committed," as we would say today. And this is precisely why he doubted – not Christ, certainly, nor the others, but himself. What was in question for him was not so much Mary Magdalen's testimony, nor that of the other ten; it was his own belief.

There was something that he had not yet been able understand. Why was it that Jesus, the son of God, needed once more to assume the human condition? Son of David, are you never to be delivered? Has not everything then been fulfilled? And yet, to deny the resurrection would be to deny the divine utterance, to deny the Word.

** *Summa theologica.*

Thus Thomas awoke to himself and knew that he was two. His soul had not ceased to believe, but it had left his body in the shadows. And inasmuch as his flesh hesitated, as his senses did not know or refused, he trembled before his destiny as an apostle; he felt helpless to bear witness in full. So evidently it was his body that he had to convince before he could go any further. "Except I shall see in his hands the print of the nails, and put my finger into the print of the nails, and thrust my hand into his side, *I will not believe*."

Thomas, the Didymus, twin of Jesus, as the Gnostics were to call him – did he not feel Christ in himself as his divine brother? In order to realize this presence fully, he needed to experience this mystery in himself, to know for himself the return of Jesus of Nazareth into his body, allowing his faith to become incarnate through the communion of sense and spirit. And at this instant, the apostle Thomas was reborn. "My Lord and my God." He was transfigured by the overflowing joy of a new encounter; for at that moment, he *met* Christ, both in his spirit and in his body.

Jesus had said to Mary Magdalen, "Touch me not." She had been the first to see him; but she "knew not that it was Jesus." Then his disciples from Emmaus had met him. He walked beside them, he spoke to them; "but their eyes were holden that they should not know him." A little later, Jesus appeared and "stood in the midst" of the disciples; "but they were terrified and affrighted, and supposed that they had seen a spirit." And he said to them: "Behold my hands and feet, that it is I myself. Handle me, and see; for a spirit hath not flesh and bones, as ye see me have." Finally, he appeared to them again on the shores of the Sea of Tiberias. There again they failed to recognize him. A miraculous haul of fish was necessary to convince them.

What they saw, and what filled them with amazement, was clearly the *body* of the Son of Man. But it was his resurrected body, his body from now on incorruptible, his "radiant body." It was he and it was not he. The great mystery was accomplished.

But there he was among them. He broke bread. He ate with them. Surely this transcends human experience. And yet it is to this rebirth that we are called, even before death. It can be given to us to experience this in our lifetime – by analogy.

But as Karl von Eckhartshausen writes: "So that this deification and transformation of earth into heaven can come about, there must be a change, a conversion of our being. This change of being, this conversion, is called rebirth.

"The rebirth is threefold: firstly, the rebirth of our *reason*. Secondly, the rebirth of our *heart* or *will*. And finally, the rebirth of our whole being.

"The first and second are *spiritual rebirths*; and the third, *corporeal rebirth*.

"Many serious men in their search for God have been reborn in intelligence and will; but few have known this rebirth of the body."

Parabola – "Corporeal rebirth" . . . There are so many things which are really the body which we call something else. I think most people think of the body as something very separate from the mind and the feelings.

Henri Tracol – Separate, yes, and even alien. Alien and despicable. I must confess I always feel distressed when I am confronted with this tendency to look down on the body. Looking down on it, and ignoring the essential part it has to play in the awakening to reality.

P. – Isn't it a question of levels?

H.T. – Indeed, but on which scale? I can think of the body as the lower part that has to be hidden and left behind, but I may also rediscover it as something that evokes a very different approach to the experience of life.

P. – But here is the problem: it *does* have to be left behind. If there is anything of more duration in us, it is going to have to get along without the body, the body as we know it. What is the real relation, then, between what we might call the body and what we might call the soul? If this evident body is going to be discarded, what will take its place? Perhaps that is what I'm asking. What is this possible "corporeal rebirth," as von Eckhartshausen puts it?

H.T. – Maybe it has something to do with recurrence.

P. – Recurrence? What do you really mean by that?

H.T. – Beyond the lure of time in succession, we have been given the idea that endlessly we come back, and come back, and come back, that we are born again and again. So, we have a sense of recurring time which can be perceived even in a very simple way through breathing in air and breathing out, through waking again and again to the alternation of day and night, the round of the seasons, and so on. Of course, there is decay and there is death, but what is my experience of rebirth? I cannot just sweep this idea away. It is something I am offered to welcome – being born again. I have been absent for hours and all of a sudden I wake up: I am born again. Where am I born again? In this body.

P. – I think my question has to do with the necessity for understanding to be incarnated. In the piece you wrote you said that the "body and its members need to participate in the knowledge which the heart and head have welcomed." Right away, one agrees and knows that it is so. At the same time one recognizes the difficulty, and resistance, and sort of darkness which the body at times can represent. Yet one knows that without that organic understanding, all knowledge is empty and without any force. I suppose I'm asking: what is the contribution of the body in understanding?

H.T. – I would say that when one is granted this awakening to a deeper reality, the body does take part in it. I cannot but appreciate the resonance of it in my body. There is something which responds quite naturally to it – it is neither invented nor imposed. It is there of its own accord. Why should I blame the body for any resistance? In fact, is it not the mind that resists?

P. – When we speak of human experience, do we speak of the physical body alone?

H.T. – The physical body alone – what does it mean? It means a crippled man in a way. There is no communication, no coming together. Maybe most human beings are like that – these millions of seeds that disappear for lack of the ferment of life. But insofar as a man is sensitive to what he is offered as a means to awaken and be part of something which gives him a new meaning, the distinction between mind, body, and feeling becomes meaningless. We are much more concerned by the *relationship* between mind and body, feeling and body, and by the presence of something that bears witness to their unity. And here again, looking down on the body has no relevance.

P. – I wonder if I understand the idea of two opposing forces and the reconciliation of those forces. Perhaps there isn't a split between the mind and body so much as a distance between them. And yet every tradition recognizes two opposing forces that do not automatically tend towards unity. In this article, too, you speak of the "laborious fusion" of opposing tendencies in oneself. But is the body at one end of the pole and the mind at the other? And if it is, isn't it necessary? Is there any movement without that initial separation?

I have been absent for hours and all of a sudden I wake up: I am born again. Where I am I born again? In this body.

H.T. – I think this is a source of many misunderstandings. There is no doubt that there is an opposition, which may be applied to mind and body; its origin, its source, however, is not mind itself, or body itself. It seems that the mind has a natural tendency to feel independent from the body. And the body is rather passive there. Now, the necessary opposition between "yes" and "no" takes advantage of this division. And we also know that it is possible not to refuse this contradiction, but to make use of it in order to go further, and to reconcile "yes" and "no" – which is not at all what we do when we look down on the body.

P. – So you would say that it is a false idea that the source of the "no" is the body and the source of the "yes" is the mind?

H.T. – It's mainly a delusion – the pretense of the mind to be superior. Both are meant to take part in a process which brings them together – a reconciliation. Otherwise, there is only an endless opposition between yes and no, yes and no.

P. – This is where the mystery is, in the relation between the two – there is a mystery in the relation between yes and no, in the relation between any two opposing forces. I was thinking of the physical body as the ground in which something can appear. And yet if I put a stone into the earth, nothing is going to appear; but if I plant a seed – what is this something in the ground and something in the seed through which the shell of the seed breaks and life appears? That is where the mystery is, isn't it? In the relation. A yes and no can oppose each other forever without bringing about a result.

H.T. – That's exactly the way I look at it. It is a mystery and I seem to ignore it when I stick to this opposition of yes and no, or body and mind, or whatever contradiction. It's a mystery which I have to respect and I have to bow to its evidence. How to awake to it? I think there is room for opening to the great miracle of nature itself. If I am moved by the vision and perception of nature – looking at the sky, looking at a tree, or any natural phenomenon – I can look at the body with the same awe and gratefulness. Then, I am given to perceive something which in itself is so great: it is a call, and I hear it.

. . . there is a recurring temptation of, I would say, dream and disincarnation . . .

P. – Yes, but it only becomes marvelous and worthy of respect when one knows that by itself it is nothing. And even the soul by itself is nothing. Isn't it so? It's only in the name of what it makes possible that it has value.

H.T. – Yes; and we may be helped by seeing how objective art makes use of the body as a subject. It is not naturalistic with emphasis on all sorts of awesome, wonderful details; the body itself is an intermediary. It bears witness to that which is far beyond our ordinary perceptions. I see how so often my mind interferes and tries to analyze. But in certain statues of the Buddha, let's say, there is a sense of oneness. Not "What is the body? What is the mind?" It is *one*. There is a sense of unity, of oneness.

I would say that when I try to come back and awake again, when I hear the call and try to answer it, I feel invited to experience *myself here, now*. I could be in China – "here" is not China – "here" is my body. And "*now*": neither yesterday, nor tomorrow. Right now, here and now . . . this is when and where mind and body come together, and I am left with the impression that there is no longer any opposition. That's what made me feel so deeply this text of von Eckhartshausen, this third possibility to welcome the rebirth *of our whole being*.

The first tendency is to discard the body. Yet at times, more subtle forces coming from an independent source, and not from the mind alone, the feeling or the body alone, can bring about their reintegration. Obviously, there is a recurring temptation of, I would say, dream and disincarnation, a dream of being free from all this. And then arises the possibility of reincarnation, with the acknowledgement of the reality of what is offered me through the perception of my body, transformed as it is by these subtle forces.

Of course, I cannot claim to "understand" what is meant by this reincarnation, but neither can I deny it. Sometimes, I come closer to a recognition of the process of creation; I feel worked on, and permeated by an impression of being born again. I'm not the master, I'm not the one who directs this – but it is granted me, I am here to receive it, and I do receive it – not passively, but taking part in it as actively as possible. It does require my participation, otherwise it passes through me but it leaves practically no trace.

P. – When you spoke before about the possibility of reincarnation, somehow you gave me the idea of a connection between that and the Christian idea of the divine incarnation.

H.T. – One can try to think about this fantastic sacrifice of God accepting to be reincarnated into a human body. That I cannot understand, but it calls for a deep wish to come closer to it. Christ accepted and assumed this incarnation, and moreover, after his death – the death of his provisional body – he even decided to come back to it . . . This is far beyond our capacity of thinking, except by analogy; I mean there are moments when I am lifted towards another sense of my own reality, another way of being, through very subtle thoughts and feelings that seem to have nothing to do with my body – until all of a sudden it opens itself to a real wish to join and take part in this experience: it reminds me of its existence and calls me back. As far as I am able to awake, and keep awake, to this call as to a genuinely objective demand, I may feel a little bit – a very little bit – closer to Christ's situation when he came back.

P. – What can you say about the real relationship between my ordinary body – my ordinary self in this body – and its relationship with this possible subtle body that it seems to recognize at moments? What is the relation?

H.T. – It cannot be understood from outside. It is like asking a craftsman: "How do you do it?" He cannot explain. He can only say: "Just try and you will see for yourself." It is not something to be spoken about, it is something to experience.

P. – It seems all of this is more possible the more open one is. The difficulty is we live most of our lives completely closed, and we start from a closed place and want to figure out how to be open – in words. How can we begin to find an approach to the body through an idea? In the last issue Kobori Roshi said that the instinctual functioning needs to be free, and a question for me is: what is a free body free from? What is it free to do – what place can it take? What is it free for?

H.T. – There is no easy answer to that. We could go deeper into the question. I am thinking of the familiar experience of looking at a landscape with somebody. I am interested in everything I see, until the other person says, "Have you noticed this or that?" No! "But look." And all of a sudden, it appears. In fact, I had seen it, but without realizing that I had. It is there as if it were not there, but it is there. And this applies to myself as well. There are times when I come back to myself, here, now. Then something else emerges, which we call memory. It's amazing, isn't it? What is there to remind me of myself when I have been swept away? The memory is there. I see there is a purpose, an intention. It is not mine: it works through me. I am reminded of what I have been granted to experience – for a purpose.

Circle, Triangle and Square.

A Born Seeker

Man is born a seeker.
Equipped as he is by nature for vibrating to a vast range of impressions, is he not predestined to an endless wondering? Bound by necessity to select from these impressions those suitable for conscious assimilation – and thereby to approach a genuine perception of his own identity – is he not singled out for continuous self-interrogation?

Such is his true vocation, his birthright. He may forget it, deny it, bury it in the depths of his unconscious being; he may go astray, misuse this hidden gift and increase his own alienation from reality; he may even try to convince himself that he has reached, once and for all, the shores of eternal Truth. No matter; this secret call is still alive, prompting him from within to try, and to try increasingly, to realize the significance of his presence here on earth. For he is here to awake, to remember and to search, again and still again.

Search for what? it could be asked. Surely there must be a definite aim, a purpose, a mark to be hit in due course. Have we not been warned only too often by modern scientists that "if you don't know *what* you are looking for, you will never know what you actually find"? According to their view, mathematical predictability must always prevail over the fertile challenge of uncertainty. And none of them will listen if you venture to remark that to "know" beforehand inevitably means that you will never "find" anything. Indeed there is no escape from the old bugbear of "whatness" unless we remember Scotus Erigena's dictum, "God does not know what He is, because He is not any 'what'."

This cannot but remind me of my last meeting with an aging friend who was about to undertake what he sensed would be his last journey to sacred places and wise men of the East.

Bidding him good-bye, I said, "I hope you will find what you are seeking." He replied with a peaceful smile, "Since I am really searching for nothing, maybe I shall find it."

Reprinted by kind permission of Jean Sulzberger, Editor of SEARCH, Harper & Row, 1979.

Let us get rid at once of a possible misunderstanding and clearly state that no real knowledge can ever be attained by mere chance. There is such fascination in the shifting lure of existence that it draws our interest away from the immediate perception of the essential. Letting oneself drift into persuasive "visions" and "discoveries", no matter how seductive, or yielding to the spell of what could be called "search for the sake of searching," is merely to indulge in daydreaming – a form of self-tyranny very much at variance with man's objective needs.

Then how is one to set about an authentic quest? Instead of surrendering at once to the call of any particular "way", one should first try with humility to discern some of the requisites for setting off on the right foot.

Is not the first essential an act of *recognition* – recognition of the utter necessity of search itself, its priority, its urgency for him who aspires to awake and assume as fully as possible his inner and outer existence?

Whenever a man awakes, he awakes from the false assumption that he has always been awake, and therefore the master of his thoughts, feelings and actions. In that moment, he realizes – and this is the shadow side of recognition – how deeply ignorant he is of himself, how narrowly dependent on the web of relationships by which he exists, how helplessly at the mercy of any suggestion that happens to act upon him at a given moment.

He may also awake – if only for a flash – to the light of a higher consciousness, which will grant him a glimpse of the world of hidden potentialities to which he essentially belongs, help him transcend his own limitations, and open the way to inner transformation.

At such a moment the call to search resounds in him and hope is born in his heart. But woe betide him if he believes himself safe from now on. The vision does not last – perhaps it is not meant to last – and once more he is left with the dizzying impression of having sunk back into his own insoluble contradictions.

Feeling lost, he may lose himself further in his search for self-recovery; experiencing his blindness, he may increase it in trying to see; becoming aware of his slavery, he may let his very search for freedom fetter him still more.

Until suddenly he awakes anew, and the whole process begins again. In the long run, by trying and failing, over and over, he may come at last to attune himself to the specific part he has to perform in this enigmatic play.

Whenever a man awakes and remembers his purpose, he awakes

to a fleeting miracle, and at the same time to an unanswerable riddle. He realizes, at moments, that in order for him to awake he was foredoomed to sleep; in order for him to remember, he was foredoomed to forget. Such is the law of this equivocal situation: without sleep, no awakening; without oblivion, no remembering. Hence, if he goes on looking for what is beyond ambivalence, it will prove to be merely another phantasm. In fact, there is, and always has been, a secret continuity in his being, which is partly reflected in the unchanging structure of his body and the regularly recurring activities of its functions. But in a perpetually moving world of energies, such a relative continuity can never be equated with immutability. The law of man's existence is to become – or to die. If a man were to stay still forever and merge into eternity, there would be little sense in his remaining here on earth.

Such is the human condition: a lucid and total acceptance of it is imperative. This alone will help the true searcher to reaffirm his inner determination. He must be ready to comply with a constantly shifting reality, ready to reconcile himself to the law of alternation, the law of successive turns of fate, ready to conform to whatever may be offered, either favorable or hostile, ready to reject all wishful thinking and to expect nothing in the way of result or reward.

Sooner or later, he will have to try not only to accept risks, but to take up the challenge *knowingly* and put himself in jeopardy. Only then will he truly respond to the call. Far from abjuring the revelations accorded him through teachings he may previously have come in contact with, he longs to "verify" them – that is, to prove them true for himself here and now. Conscious participation in what is self-evident is the goal of the geniune searcher: a goal so close and at the same time so remote, a goal so constantly offered and again withheld – in order that he may keep on searching.

For a man, far beyond his personal hopes and predilections, to search is a sacred task, and if he assents to it and persistently endeavours to fulfill it, he will experience it as truly corresponding both to his essential needs and to his specific capacities.

Patience – much patience, endurance and determination, watchfulness and readiness, availability and conscious flexibility – all these are indispensable to the seeker.

Maybe the time will come when he realizes that in order to develop these latent potentialities he needs guidance and support. Freed from any pretension to be a "knower", he will deliberately put himself under the authority of a master. To absorb his teachings and follow his directives? Yes, and even more important, to perceive and to study the way he deals with life and people, to watch how he conveys his understanding through behavior and tone of voice, and, ultimately, to be able to receive his wordless glance.

By serving such an apprenticeship the seeker gradually unbinds himself from prejudice and becomes sensitive to a wide range of manifestations or testimonies of search, wherever he may happen upon them – and this regardless of any apparent inconsistencies he encounters between their respective features. He will realize that they all refer to the same Unknown that he himself confronts.

With this in mind, one may ask oneself why Sengai's eloquent drawing has been chosen as the motif for this book. Does not this Zen picture appear as a concluding gesture to what must have been, for the artist, a lifelong search? We cannot help visualizing Sengai preparing himself – hours of meditation in perfect stillness – then the smooth and careful stirring of the ink, and the brush rises, remains for a moment suspended in the air like an eagle watching its prey, until, all of a sudden – lo – it is done!

Circle, triangle, square.

But what kind of a geometrician is this man? Look at his "square"! The inaccuracy of the lines, the faintness of the ink! But Sengai, obviously, does not care: ordinary exactitude is no part of his province. Clearly, he is more concerned with the inner relationship among the three symbols and the way they engender one another.

Their sequence in itself is a riddle. If we ponder upon it, we realize that it naturally flows from right to left. Following the movement of the brush, we complete the circle, leave it for the triangle, and finally vanish into the last stroke of the square.

For us, it may be difficult to accept this interpretation of the sequence, since according to our Western system of associations, we automatically see it moving from left to right. That is the way we are trained to "read" things, reaching always towards the full stop and the closing of the circle.

There exist, in fact, reliable hints as to Sengai's probable intention. Professor D. T. Suzuki, the noted authority on Zen Buddhism, has suggested that the *circle* represents formlessness, emptiness or the void where there is yet no separation of light and darkness; the *triangle* evokes the birth of form out of formlessness; and the *square*, as a combination of two opposite triangles, stands for the multiplicity of things.

From the infinite oneness down to the inexhaustible variety of forms in which it divides itself, from the secrecy of Essence to the everspringing Manifestation, here lies the mystery of involutive

Creation.

But should we rest satisfied with Suzuki's marvelously condensed vision as the only reliable one? Or would such an easy consent not, in a sense, betray both painting and comment? Rather, we should keep our minds open to the flow of suggestions that comes from other sources, for instance the "squaring of the circle" of the Alchemists – and even those that may arise from our own inner recesses – while making sure that we do not fall under the spell of any of them.

Are we now ready to transcend the dangerous fascination of apparent contradictions?

Let us ponder the order given to the three sections of *Search* and the way it has been designed to tally with the left-to-right pattern. Here again, we are faced with the law of alternation, for now is the time to climb back to the source. Having been exiled to this small, remote planet, where our only possible chance of survival requires the protective ramparts of material stability *(square)*, we have to find our way laboriously to the discovery of direction, guidance and consistency *(triangle)* until we are ready for the ultimate quest – the return to the origin, the beginning *(circle)*, from where . . . but that is another story, or rather, perhaps the same story, the one everlasting story.

For the born searcher there is no escape from the labyrinth. Perhaps he will even realize that he himself is the labyrinth, and that no failure, no "answer" offered along the way, will ever stop him from moving further toward the centre of his own mystery. And, far from trying to evade the challenge, he will hope to become more and more able to meet it: this alone will confer meaning upon his search.

Birth of a Sculpture

H.T. – In order to avoid any misunderstanding, let me say that I am not a professional sculptor: I haven't studied at any school of fine arts or even taken part in workshops. At best, I've received some helpful advice from sculptor friends who have encouraged me to follow what I might well describe as a kind of *calling*.

Certainly I have the greatest respect for the *craft*, for its rules, its standards, its requirements – its tools, equipment, etc. – and of course above all for the material, for the substance itself, which is not in any way to be violated, destroyed, or reduced to nothing, but on the contrary, is to be called to life, its own life.

What does this still, silent block of stone wish to say? It is as if it were waiting for me in order to find through me its true form. And when I ask myself this question, another question is bound to echo in me: what is it that "I" wish to say, what is the meaning of my presence on earth, what meaning can I discover in this unknown presence, in this unknown that I am?

Q. – Then we could say that art is self-knowledge – and also that self-knowledge is an art?

H.T. – Without a doubt. It is an art which has its own laws, laws which cannot be broken. But I am systematically anti-systematic; I am always careful not to fall in the trap of "thinking I understand" just because I have had a glimmering of certain ideas which are quite plausible but which have not been part of my experience.

To be precise, I believe the most important thing here is to *enter into the experience*, to feel that one is the material on which all sorts of relatively independent forces are acting. What is it that allows me to be in a certain way the sculptor of myself, or at least to cooperate with the forces that shape me? If I don't do that, I am letting these forces operate and make whatever they wish of me. But something in me is called on; as a human being, I am invited to take part in my own

Answers to the questions of a journalist on Pierre Descargues' programme, Le Monde au Singulier televised by the France Culture network, 1981. Translated by the late D. M. Dooling and published in PARABOLA magazine Vol. XVI, No. 3, 1991 on Craft. Reprinted here by kind permission of the Editors.

formation. And perhaps it is that which reinforces my interest in self-knowledge through the experience of art – not an intellectual interest but one that is much more profound and comes from a deeper source.

Q. – How would you relate this very self-knowledge, this immersion in the experience that you just spoke of, with what is called the theory of knowledge? How can one find one's way there?

H.T. – How can one find one's way – perhaps a whole lifetime would not be enough for that. But it is possible to search, to search honestly. We are led astray by images of what we thought we understood from reading books and listening to "experts". I need to feel that I am directly concerned, that again and again I give myself to the task as immediately as possible, whether or not I apply it to working on a sculpture. I try to make myself available in such a way that I can be conscious of the forces that pass through me, in order to understand better their direction and orientation, and adapt myself better to them; to try more effectively to become a good instrument – and a conscious one.

Here the mystery reappears: how can I be a conscious instrument of the forces which pass through me and determine what I am? How can I be a workman in this work which is in process, at the same time *knowing* it, with a nascent autonomy, with something which truly obliges me to try to see what corresponds best with what my real self calls me to be?

There is a sentence from Elie Faure which has haunted me since my adolescence, that echoes what I have just tried to say: "The only man who adds to the spiritual wealth of humanity is the one who has the strength to become what he is."

Individual Culture: its possibilities and its demands

"**W**hat do I know?"
Rather than hiding behind a screen of smiling scepticism to avoid any answer, this question can well up in a man as a moment of truth when, reflecting on his life, he wakes up to the urgency of an inner search.

If he questions himself in all simplicity, what pre-occupies him, it seems, is not so much the obvious poverty of his knowledge but, far more, his capacity to understand the nature and deep meaning of his relationship with the outer world, with his fellow men and with himself.

In fact, the "culture" foisted on him since childhood and which surrounds him on all sides, exerts a tyrannical pressure on his natural aspirations: for some two hundred years free rein has been given to "libido sciendi", to this appetite for knowledge freed from any religious taboo and reinforced by the will to power and material domination, flinging us peremptorily towards this nightmarish accumulation of information which is only too ready to overwhelm us.

Can any comprehensive view survive in us beneath this avalanche? Contrary to the pictures we might have of one or other of past great civilisations, there is nothing monolithic about contemporary culture. Beneath a surface uniformity, appropriate for ensuring the necessary exchanges between types of societies with very different ethnic and social pre-dominances, cultural reality is necessarily multi-form – as many sociologists and anthropologists nowadays do not fail to point out.

Furthermore, how not to take into account the natural range of social strata at the heart of every nation, whose mental, emotional and physical imperatives so often reveal enormous rifts and incompatibilities between them? It is therefore no longer permissible to talk endlessly about culture in general as if it were one indivisible entity.

What, then, are we looking for? If culture cannot be acquired once and for all, if, on the contrary, it invites us periodically to a review and

(Lecture given in 1961 in Mexico City under the auspices of the Instituto Nacional de Antropologia e Historia)

to a merciless criticism of all that seemed until then answerable, what fanciful notions does it incite us to pursue? The demand nevertheless is there, and since we cannot dissociate ourselves from this collection of contradictory data which conditions us on all sides, we might as well opt for an attempt to adjust to the ongoing processes, to a conscious participation in the very life of this disconcerting phenomenon in order to have a better grasp of its multiple parts.

After all, we know only too well the futility of any attempt to confine forever this moving reality to one 'definitive' concept, as if one could put an end to the vital function of adaptation by means of which from century to century humanity ponders upon its adventure.

But we must not deceive ourselves: to recognise this necessity, to restore the essential role of the individual in the awareness and development of a living culture, is tantamount to a certain boldness, a need to take an active part in it – whereas everything invites us, nowadays, to let ourselves be carried along . . .

"Just get born – and we'll take care of the rest!" This slogan of a powerful Californian insurance company proclaiming that it will take charge, in advance, of all the risks of our existence, sums up marvellously the cultural perspectives which are nowadays offered to us.

Is *no* effort asked of us? Of course it is.

But any effort is nowadays considered a constraint from which it is advisable to free oneself as quickly as possible – as is suggested perfectly by the poster of the smiling man opening the door of his new car to a pretty woman with the caption: "Life begins at five in the afternoon". At one minute past five you leave the office; relax without further ado. The only thing you have to do is to let yourself go.

Letting oneself go: the ultimate in laziness and passivity. From docile producer bowing to necessity, man has become the perfect consumer. In this way the worries and problems of tomorrow are automatically resolved: this 'spectre of idleness' which, it is said, threatens the worker, together with an all-powerful technology, ensures his comfort. This general invitation to inertia makes us, irresistibly, a prey to the most flagrant and most insidious influences: advertising, mass media, cinema, television . . . on all sides all of us can see ourselves conditioned by these things even in the most private part of our lives. In Indiana a marriage bureau, equipped with the latest scientific gadgets, asks its clients to fill out a questionnaire and to undergo psychological tests. The cards are punched at once, sorted out by the computer and put together; in a matter of seconds, the ideal match appears. For the last three years over 5,000 mathematically guaranteed happy marriages have been arranged . . . Only time will tell!

Yes, I know . . . we had better watch out or, before we know where we are, we will be accused of fighting a rearguard action in favour of an outmoded individualism.

In reality we have not the slightest intention of giving free rein to any old elementary defensive reaction, but the very opposite: to try to understand better the real situation of the individual in society. And our first task is to recognise that what it would be tempting to describe as pseudo-cultural aggression, is nothing less than a wild, abusive and uncontrolled proliferation of the natural and necessary process of compulsory education.

But this is just the point: even the most frivolous approach to educational problems highlights how indispensable it is to awaken in everyone, from childhood on, that movement of withdrawal, of standing back to question and ponder what is proposed, in order to counterbalance adequately the tendency to passive acceptance and blind conformity. There is nothing more moving than the sight, at school or at home, of the first appearance of the strength to resist the natural authority of the social or family milieu and of an opening to the spirit of questioning and of independent search, thanks to which the sense of his own responsibility can affirm itself and later develop in an individual. Alas, more often than not, no sooner has this new feeling of himself appeared in a child than it is immediately concealed, veiled in clothing which is lent to him as if all those round him had been seized with panic at the sight of his seeming nakedness.

Later, of course, when he reaches adolescence, he will be provided with the practical means, the wherewithal, and even the pretence of his emancipation in such a way that in trying to affirm himself as an autonomous being, all he does is to reflect, unwittingly, by his subjectivity, a model of the surrounding social milieu.

Decade after decade, it seems, this situation evolves; contemporary man has at his disposal more and more ways to check out for himself the copious material of knowledge which never stops being offered to him. But in the long run, just because of his ever widening field of experience, his limitations only succeed in revealing themselves more and more.

Take, for example, the field of scientific discoveries: from very early on a division of labour among research workers imposed itself as an absolute necessity, in such a way that, in order to proceed with his work according to the rules of the game, any specialist has to rely on a lot of other specialists and trust them fully, since he has not got the means to verify directly the merits of their conclusions.

Any scientist who is considered an authority in his own field is a layman among his peers in other domains. So what about all the others who simply long to get some sort of idea of what is going on?

This difficulty of going beyond the narrow frontiers of our ordinary perceptions is indeed not new. What is the difference, for example, between, on the one hand, our flagrant incapacity to encompass the information that the light of our closest star, Alpha Centauri, takes four years to reach us, and, on the other hand, the reaction of the Athenians when they wondered whether Anaxagoras was joking when he suggested that the sun was at least as large as the Peloponnese?

Faced with the dizzying perspectives opened up by contemporary science as well as the technical prowess at our disposal, we find ourselves in a situation not unlike that of so-called "primitive" peoples when we invite them to share the material advantages of our civilisation. Likewise it is not absolutely indispensable to have a knowledge, albeit slight, of the theory of the four-stroke engine in order to drive the latest model on the improvised motorways of Central Africa.

And what to make of the following story?

Somewhere, in the Northern Territory of Canada the military authorities had to recruit a number of local Eskimos, huntsmen and fishermen, to help build an air base. They were given a basic training for four months after which they were able to be successfully employed in the various activities of the site. What with high salaries, comfortable bungalows, equipped with television, heating and other amenities, in no time they adapted themselves to the ways of their employers. I am not sure how long this went on for, but one fine day, it was decided in high circles to transfer the air base some hundred kilometers away. Since it was out of the question to take the Eskimos too, they were abandoned on the deserted site, with a few kind words and sage advice . . . But all in vain: to go back to their "igloos" seemed quite impossible; apparently they had forgotten how to hunt or fish and they had no wish to return to the past. They stubbornly shut themselves up in their houses without water or electricity. Some months later, when a military detachment happened to visit the place on an inspection tour, these Eskimos were found dead from starvation and the cold.

Thus our generous offer to so-called "under-developed people" to come and reap the benefits of the wondrous acquisitions of our civilisation has turned out to be, for them, at the end of the day, a truly wretched affair. For the sake of transistors and pocket calculators they exchange what was most precious for them – a way of living duly adapted to the specific conditions of their natural environment, in harmony with their own culture and their sense of taking part in the life of the universe.

Putting aside all sentimentality let us try to learn from this lesson.

When a way of life entirely devoted to the fascinating illusion of unlimited material progress is offered to us we should stop for a moment before yielding to temptation. There cannot be a definite answer either way – for or against – but only a *conditional, a tentative* one. We need, at least, to know the score and if the act of participation in this giddy race means giving up the search for a more direct awareness of my relationship with the life of the universe, I can only say No, I do not want to die of cold and exhaustion in this interior waste land.

For the danger is well and truly there: the future seems to be exploding all round us at the speed of a rocket blasting off. But from the moment a man realises this he alone becomes responsible for his destiny: he alone can choose between mechanical conformity or the attitude of determination required for his own development. If the truth be told, many of us feel overwhelmed – saturated even – by the deluge of ever new propositions. Some succumb to a sort of nihilism and a terrifying laxity. Some try to forget their surroundings and seek refuge either in the past or some other quixotry.

Some try to compensate by hiding behind specialisations, but at the end of the day it is very clear that something other than a flimsy screen is required to protect us from this invasion. It can be confronted with honesty only with a clear-sighted, supple, discriminating vigilance – a watchfulness, which is asking to be "cultivated" We must not forget: social in its origins as well as in its temporal finality, culture is essentially an individual phenomenon. It has to do with an inner demand which requires an arduous labour to which not everybody can submit. From the outset the seeker must be ready to weigh up everything, question everything again and again.

There is no individual culture without the individual. And *who* is he?

Here we have to admit that the idea of the "individual" has, since the beginning of the century, undergone the same sort of upheaval as the atom. Indivisible as it was believed to be, it gradually appeared as a world of another level, in the depths of which the incredible dance of the elementary particles goes on and on.

In the same way, in the eyes of we explorers of our unconscious depths, it would seem that the human being cannot find a single gesture, a single word, a single thought, a single way of feeling, the roots of which in the last analysis could not be found deeply embedded in the recent or distant past of humanity.

It is clear that, as it turns out, the so-called individual has, nowadays, a very questionable "individuality". In reality he does not exist in his own right, but as an already established network of relationships which determine him at each moment, and as a combination of potentialities yet to be realised. He is no more than a promise – a promise of himself, and who then will fulfil this promise?

This more or less chaotic aggregate of inclinations and pre-dispositions naturally suggests an act of creative consciousness, so that the autonomous structure can at least reveal its outline.

Now, beyond the reciprocal and always increasing resistance of our sensory, motor, mental and emotional faculties, each of us can always perceive in ourselves an essential tendency to unity, which bears witness to our analogy to the Whole. When he becomes aware of this, the potential individual perceives within himself the possibilities of a centre of understanding round which can gravitate the various diffuse and contradictory elements of his being.

It is in this manner that the real meaning of the "universal" – literally what is "oriented towards unity" – re-discovers itself in him.

Without this immediate perception of the universal, any claim to "universality" is, in fact, a misuse of language. Obviously we are not referring here to the necessary uniformity of technical equipment, nor to the unavoidable task of establishing a basic cultural ground for a platform of communications and exchanges on a planetary scale. For, although justified and imperative in their aim, there is nevertheless a dimension missing there.

The universality we are speaking about has nothing to do with rationalist expansion. It is an inner certainty which is common to all those who re-discover their own, proper identity with the universe and which knows no temporal or spatial frontiers: it *is* – at all times and in all places.

"Each man carries within himself the entire form of the human condition", said Montaigne. Three and a half centuries later Jung joins him in his own way with this concept of the "collective unconscious" which is present in all of us. Despite the reservations that we could formulate with regard to his terminology, there is no doubt that, with his idea of archetypes, Jung has re-opened a perspective that had been forgotten for a long time: a perspective which, as long as we do not stop halfway, restores to man his true stature, filling his inner firmament with powerful constellations. In his dark night, inhabited by forgotten symbols, he who wishes to know himself must deliberately open his eyes and become aware of the powers he is connected with, feel himself in harmony with and try to comply with them. This is the real meaning of an individual culture: to acknowledge and choose his true destiny and then fulfil it. Then the individual appears as the author and creator of his inner world . . . so true is it that the original meaning of the word "author" is "one who makes grow" . . . An authority which does not encourage growth, that does not awaken the interest and the wish to raise oneself up, very soon turns into a petty tyranny and a meaningless code of behaviour.

In order to create its proper world, authority demands more than a blind submission: it is indispensable that it should inspire a wish to draw nearer to it and fuse with it, in order to understand better how to be at the service of what it represents. It is not enough to claim to know. Authority must be sought for and acknowledged. And really, if I do not acknowledge the presence of an authority in myself I will have no possibility whatsoever of finding it outside myself.

I find it, I lose it. I find it again and unceasingly I put it to the test. I put it in doubt to assure myself of my understanding and with the aim of acknowledging it again with ever more conviction.

Here lies the reconciliation between authority and search: they need each other. They attract one another mutually in this movement of unending renewal through which the life of culture perpetuates itself.

Anyway, we know very well the final aim of the individual does not rest with him, but with his conscious participation in the destiny of all mankind, and these would be hollow words if an actual movement in this direction were not already visible: here and there, small groups of seekers are gathering together with the single aim of concentrating their efforts towards a common understanding of the return to the essential.

"What do I know?"

Whoever ponders seriously this question understands little by little his relation with "Who am I?", echoes of which resound down the centuries since man first appeared on this planet.

For these seekers, *to be*, *to know* and *to do* are the facets of the same reality. To dream of knowing oneself and nothing more, without looking for the slightest hint of an intentional manifestation fully integrated with the surrounding reality, is tantamount to a kind of desertion. As for trying "to do" without being aware of "being", without looking at every step for a way to be in accord with an inner presence, is the worst kind of abdication. The human condition is a perpetual challenge, which man cannot ignore without abandoning his true nature.

He who wakes up to the deep meaning of his life and perceives how he makes room for the force and the difficulties of the innumerable relationships offered to him, acknowledges, by the same token, the very point of his existence. He discovers the possibility of seizing hold of the present, in order to bring together in a supreme effort the unfathomable experience of the past with the immediate prospects for the future, for which he wishes to feel himself responsible.

Taking into consideration his potentialities as well as his limitations, choosing the best influences for him, he has for aim *to work always according to his being*, in order to affirm himself at each moment, in constant submission to the demands of the life of the universe.

This would be the authentic *art of living* and the visible manifestation of a real individual culture.

L.D. – What is the fault you despise most in others?

H.T. – Small-mindedness – in all its forms. Its smell – in myself as in others – unleashes in me more than contempt – nausea. A healthy revolt. "The anger of the just man." But as for small-minded people, I strive to feel for them nothing but an active sympathy. I should so much like to be able to unbind their swaddling clothes, help them to stretch their limbs, thaw them out, compel them at all costs to look further than the end of their own noses, to take a deep breath and throw themselves into the current.

And I am angry with myself for not knowing how to go about it – or for not daring to – small-minded myself!

In Search of a Living Culture: present perspectives of culture and the problem of universality

Whether a history graduate or a tabloid reader, a jet-pilot or author of a treatise on phenomenology, each one of us, in one way or another, is part of the culture of our country and our time. We are impregnated by it, we take part in it. We live it.

This most subtle, most essential nourishment which we expect, most often without knowing it, to make sense of our lives, is meted out to us even before we are born.

Myriads of images, risen from the depths, secretly direct the interest we will bring to the natural and the human surroundings in the midst of which we are called to live. Then the influences of all kinds, exercised on us in turn by the family circle, education, professional and social relationships, will determine in us the governing lines of our thoughts and feelings and even the form of our experiences.

Why, then, would we go looking for what pervades us and surrounds us on all sides?

To tell the truth, most of the time we are not that bothered anyway. We ignore the question and would even find it hard to explain clearly what we mean by "culture". And if ever we do wake up to this latent need to understand, inherent to our species; if ever we do apply ourselves to focus on the data of the problem, we will first of all seek out a *definition* of culture.

Of course, it is not definitions which are lacking: we will be offered a whole range of them, each putting the accent on such and such an aspect of this vast phenomenon to the exclusion of others; each one – as Leibnitz would say – being "true in what it affirms, false in what it denies."

There are some who even endeavour to establish a synthesis of these contradictory formulae. But here it is most often a question of arbitrary, artificial attempts which remain slaves of logical thinking obstinately glued to their principles.

To define – that would in a way put an end to the debate, to the search, *finish* with it. But, thank God, one cannot define culture for the

(*Lecture given in 1961 at Aix-en-Provence at the invitation of La Société d'Etudes Philosophiques*)

simple reason that there is nothing "final" about it. We are swept
along in its currents where it dances and whirls round and round
before once again finding its impetus. To lovers of classification,
culture leaves only traces of its passage.

Like any living entity, culture only perpetuates itself by endless
efforts of adaptation, of renewal, by alternating between apparent
death and resurrection and cannot be reduced to any one of the
transitory formulae which it might assume with the passing of
time.

Even if some of its elements have offered at times an astonishing
resistance to the assault of the centuries – as the examples of India and
China prove to us through the numerous upsets in their history –
transpositions and adjustments are still necessary in each new epoch,
so that all in all culture cannot be envisaged as an independent and
immutable reality.

It is therefore *in its becoming* and in its driving relationships that
we need to try to grasp its meaning.

We will say to begin with that the periodic decay of culture
characterises itself by a sclerosis of the *existing* possibility of
comprehension; an incapacity to display new relationships with
meaning; and that the effective presence of a culture reveals itself, on
the contrary, by the existence of a network of conceptual relationships
supple enough to guarantee a certain continuity to the totality of
individual and collective behaviour within a given society.

In what way then is culture distinguishable from civilisation?

If Paul Mus, in his semantic course at the Collège de France, takes
pains to be precise about their respective roles, it is to underline better
their complementariness.

> "Culture," he said, "is the ensemble of the
> images which perceive, illuminate and
> transmit the semantic system of a civilisation."

According to him, culture would therefore be, above all, an
awareness and a choice of meanings, and civilisation would be that
projection into action through which society takes shape. Between
these two poles a circuit is established, determined by the inevitable
gap between the conceived idea and its realisation.

Through intuition and reflection, then by intentional elaboration,
the daily reality of a society is in a way absorbed, assimilated, then
re-thought,' "re-signified". A new vision of the world emerges, which
translates itself by an "educational conditioning", producing proper
tendencies and impulses for determining new forms of behaviour and
conduct. In this way culture and civilisation beget each other.

What is appealing about this proposition is that it offers us a phenomenological description of the cultural process rather than enclosing it in an exhaustive formula. It helps us to keep the question open and burning like the crater of an active volcano.

And in effect far from appeasing our need to understand, this way of seeing culture as a permanent question will only enliven it, for, having recognised the necessity for this driving intelligence at the heart of society, we will feel our way towards the search for the laws whic govern its interventions. For lack of a global view, we will have to content ourselves with thinking round the problem as best we can by approaching it from all sides. It is anyway not entirely by chance that we will adopt this method, for, in its dynamism, it corresponds precisely to the original meaning of the word "culture".

The Indo-European root of this word is actually *k(w)el*, which contains essentially the idea of *circulating, turning around* and which is given to us notably by the Greek "circle" and "cycle" and their derivatives, but also, by the Latin *colere* (which means to inhabit a place, to dwell, hence "colony"), the words "cult", "culture" and their derivatives.

Now, if we pay some attention to it, what comes out of this lightning-trip to the sources of language, is not a simple curio of a philological order, but a conceptual scheme which we would be wrong to under-estimate.

"To turn around" implies a pivot, an axis, a centre of attraction. It is a movement of a circular kind, which tends towards its ideal form without ever fully realising it. The existence, at least virtual, of a centre – which, moreover, can itself move – constitutes the one constant in the system.

In order not to lose touch with this possible interpretation of the original meaning, if we try, with this in mind, to represent to ourselves what we are accustomed to call nowadays the cultural phenomenon, we will have to ask ourselves in the first place "around *what* does it turn?"

An elementary question maybe, but, for all that, primordial. In its essence moreover it does not seem that difficult to answer. Towards what would the cultural effort tend if not towards knowledge?

Let us understand each other here: I said towards knowledge, not towards *learning*, the accumulation of *learning* which corresponds, on the contrary, to an absolutely centrifugal tendency.

In this connection, the pleasing lines of Mathias Lubeck, a somewhat forgotten poet from between the two world wars, come to mind.

"Doctor Faust wanted to know everything.
He was damned, the story goes.
It does not look as if God wanted
To encourage public learning".

Moreover, with all due respect to our dear poet, if Faust had wanted to know everything, in a strictly quantative sense, he would not have needed God to damn him!

To learn by heart all the articles in an Encylopedia, "to become knowledgeable" is a childish dream which brings a smile to the lips. Unfortunately it often haunts, unbeknownst to us, the adults we claim to have become . . .

But Faust aspires not so much to learning as to real, central knowledge. He dreams of being in possession of the secret of secrets, the magic formula which will allow him to embrace in the twinkling of an eye the immensity of the domains accessible to science. That is his "sin." For if knowledge is one, it implies the perfect identification of subject and object of which Hindu teachings, Meister Eckhart and the great mystics of Islam speak – which excludes any claim to monopolise or *possess* them.

In this sense, all that remains open is the lightning experience of an immediate participation in knowledge in its indivisible totality, of a communion through intellectual intuition, that is to say by stepping momentarily beyond the frontiers of the interior within which our mind moves.

Knowledge, then, appears, most of the time, as out of reach, elusive in itself, absolutely unthinkable, but nevertheless capable of fostering in us an immense desire to approach it. And it is precisely its inaccessibility which makes it this permanent magnetic pole which we were evoking just now, which exercises on us its double power of attraction and repulsion in order to keep us in the field of forces which gravitate round it.

There was a time when any allusion to a transcendental reality was considered to be "not the done thing", or out of fashion, to say the least. But fashion, by its nature is ephemeral and it is no longer possible today – faced with the testimonies of learned men who, in their field, are doing their best to break the framework of a rationalism which, as of now, is out-of-date – to shrug our shoulders in such cases, for the research of contemporary physicists is going, quite literally, towards a new *meta*-physics.

Wasn't Wolfgang Pauli, by opening such fecund perspectives on nuclear science with his enigmatic "principle of exclusion", the first to own that he sees no logical justification in it and that this postulation remains in itself inexplicable by scientific thought?

And is it not disturbing to learn that the ponderings of an Einstein or an Oppenheimer have brought them closer to the Upanishads or to the Tao-Teh-Ching than to any modern philosphical treatise?

To quote just one example, here is what Oppenheimer wrote in his book: *Science and Common Understanding*:

> "To questions which seem very simple, we are
> going to give no answer, or to give one which,
> at first sight, makes one think of some strange
> catechism rather than the categorical
> affirmations of physics.
> When we are asked, for example, if the
> position of the electron remains the same, we
> should reply *"no"*; when we are asked if it
> varies in the course of time, we should reply
> *"no"*; when we are asked if the electron is
> immobile, we should again say, *"no"*; and
> when we are asked if is in movement, we
> should always reply *"no"*."

And Oppenheimer adds: "If Buddha, questioned about the states of the human individual after death, gave answers entirely of this kind, these hardly agree with the traditions of science in these last centuries."

This renouncement of classical norms of scientific speculation will naturally have profound repercussions on the destinies of culture in our time and we will have to come back to this.

But is there not above all an immense promise in the recognition of a possible analogy between the way of thinking imposed nowadays by those at the forefront of nuclear physics and that of the mystics and great sages of all time? Far more than a discovery or a conquest of the "progressive" spirit it would, then, be a question, under a new form, of an unhoped-for return to an essential step, common to the most diverse cultural elites throughout the ages and across the continents, in such a manner that one would be tempted to see in it the first fruits of a *universality* freed at last from any kind of spatial-temporal slavery and because of that even more real, even more effective.

Isn't that, moreover, the only true universality which, the very word itself tells us, is wholly turned towards *the one* and can only be understood innerly?

It makes fun of the contradictions to which the extreme differentiation of external forms give rise, knowing that they remain united in this centre, in effect, from which each one of them proceeds.

Contrarily, the current idea of universality remains peripheral and centrifugal. It tends towards the complete uniformising of fundamental human ideas by an excessive diffusion – thanks to the most recent technological advances. People are talking very seriously of using artificial satellites which, receiving huge loads of information of all kinds, will have the task of re-transmitting them continually to the public and private television aerials of the entire world! This intensive cultural bombardment would impose before long a perfect indentity between all the civilisations on the planet, so successfully that one sole and unique *Weltanschauung* would finally reign upon earth.

But why stop, then, on such a right path? Won't this latest scientific realisation be threatened in its turn, sooner or later, by the undefined expansion which, as of now, is promised to us by the space adventure and shouldn't we be thinking already of some gigantic cultural unification of the solar system? That's something which would assure in the most unexpected way the revenge of "geo-centrism" formerly victim of the Copernican revolution.

In fact, this tendency towards universality does not date from yesterday. It seems to be one of the constituent characteristics of many societies. It originates in this collection of solid certainties by which the social group affirms its autonomy. Later on it willingly takes on the form of a cultural imperialism even if it entails retiring strangely into itself if opposed, thus generating a categorical ostracism and throwing to the outer darkness anything which resists its influence. From which the idea of "barbarians" comes – "barbarians" often considered by "civilised" peoples as non-human beings, whom it was consequently permissible to reduce to slavery.

But can we be sure we have escaped from this distressing inclination? Our attitude towards the ancient past, as well as to what remains of it in non-Western societies (or where westernisation has not yet accomplished the intended rhythm) could easily make us doubt it. To our eyes, isn't civilisation exclusively what corresponds to the latest stage of *our* material and intellectual development, under the sign of a "progress" which tends to impose itself on all continents, repressing outwardly as well as inwardly the "relics" of a way of thinking henceforth reserved for "times past"?

It is specially so in the case of those Eastern cultures which are still putting up some resistance to the tidal wave coming from the West.

A man shaped by Western culture, since he was brought up in England by an English mother, that great Orientalist, Coomeraswamy, who died a few years ago in Boston, where he had been curator

of the outstanding Oriental department of the Museum of Fine Arts,
devoted the greater part of his work to shedding light on the profound
reasons for the divorce between East and West.

> "In all its diversity," he wrote in 1932, "Asia
> remains nevertheless a living spiritual unity
> which embraces, at the very least, half the
> cultural heritage of humanity.
> Nevertheless the habit persists in Europe of
> writing and compiling histories of art or of
> philosophy which make implicit claims to
> universality, whereas in fact their contents
> refer only to European history. What is known
> in general about Asia is, at best, only a series of
> sparse facts, seemingly arbitrary, for want of
> having been revealed in their relation to a
> human will. It is consequently obvious that the
> true discovery of Asia represents for most
> people an unprecedented adventure. Yet,
> without some knowledge of Asia no
> civilisation can reach maturity, no individual
> can consider himself as "civilised" nor even be
> clearly aware of what properly belongs to
> him."

And this is absolutely true: the forgetting of the essentially
cyclical character of time, the illusion of an indefinite progress on all
levels, and the conviction of therefore belonging to the most
"advanced" period in the history of humanity, long determined a
"superiority complex" in the Westerner of the 19th and early 20th
century – a complex which falsified from the outset his vision of
antiquity as well of (in his eyes) "un-civilised" peoples.

However, that is no longer the case. Lévy-Bruhl himself, who
formerly viewed with the same eye the superstitions of certain
degenerate small tribes and the great Chinese, Hindu or
pre-Colombian cosmogonies, considering them all as manifestations
of the famous "pre-logical" or "primitive" thinking, even Lévy-Bruhl
seems, in his last notebooks, published since his death, to have come
to a profound change of attitude.

Now that is something which invites us to revise certain
stereotyped judgements in regard to social phenomena which have
either been badly interpreted or hastily reduced to their most aberrant
form.

We will be helped in this by the new generation of ethnographers

and sociologists who, thanks to several pioneers, have found the
ground swept clean of a good number of pseudo-scientific taboos.
Their horizon has broadened. For them culture cannot simply be
assimilated into the ready-made stock ideas on which one kind of
civilisation is based: "culture" is, properly speaking, *a way of life*. As an
active principle it joins with civilization and constitutes thus an inner
order whose profound unity finds itself once again on all levels of
manifestation including the humblest activities of the individual.

Such a sudden change was, of course, a long way from
influencing the whole of the thinking of our contemporaries. In her
book *Patterns of Culture*, published in 1934, Ruth Benedict was still able
to say:

"The white man knows, as it were, nothing
about the ways of life which are not his own.
The world-wide diffusion of Western
civilisation has protected him better than ever
before from having to take seriously that of
other peoples. The uniformity of behaviour
and the general outlook which he sees are
prevalent everywhere seem to him sufficiently
convincing and he accepts without further ado
the idea of a simple equivalence between
human nature and his own cultural
standards."

In order to shake off the contemptuous ignorance and prejudices
which still exist in contemporary man, a certain disorientation seems
necessary at the outset. He needs to feel the full blast of a gale force
wind and to submit to the shock of enquiry, which runs counter to all
his habitual ways of thinking and his ethical beliefs. If his instinct for
preservation, or concern for his intellectual comfort do not hinder him
too much, he has some chance of then discovering in himself an echo
of these ways of thinking and of feeling which are so unfamiliar to
him, and which will resound in him not as a menacing frustration but,
the very opposite, as an enrichment, a broadening of his field of
experience.

However, we are not talking about dilettantism here. We will
leave to their past-times, their hobbies, the lovers of the exotic who
collect strange customs and unusual behaviour which come in handy
for spicing up a drawing-room conversation, or the latter-day
romantic who escapes into the dream of returning to "the state of
nature" among whimsical primitives.

No. If the exploration of other cultures is really necessary it is in order to become more aware of what our own might truly be and to clarify what, here and now, could serve as a basis for a way of life proper for our times.

> "The first condition for a discussion on
> culture," says Ruth Benedict, "is to base it on a
> wide selection of cultural forms. For us that is
> the only way to distinguish between the forms
> of social adaptation which are particular to
> local cultural type and those which are
> common to the entire human race."

What is striking indeed to the seeker, is this extreme diversity of cultures. The fundamental necessities of existence in society provoke here and there so many contradictory responses that it seems to forbid any hope of synthesis or reconciliation.

Among the numerous examples of this diversity one of the most striking concerns warfare, whose motivating forces, objectives and methods offer, in different nations, startling contrasts:

> "War can be, as it was for the Aztecs, a way of
> capturing victims for religious sacrifices.
> According to this principle the Spaniards who
> were fighting to wipe out their enemies were
> violating the rules of war in an *unintelligible*
> fashion."

Doubtless we will have as much trouble in understanding the well-known principle of "potlatch", formerly practised by the Kwakiutl of British Columbia, whose economics were based entirely on expenditure and out-bidding for the benefit of a prestige which seems to us bordering on megalomania:

> "Chief Kwakiutl made use of two methods to
> be sure of victory over his rival. One was to
> humiliate him by making him gifts of a value
> superior to anything the latter could hope to
> pay back. The other consisted in a total
> destruction of all his possessions. It was a
> challenge. And if the rival wished to avoid
> being shamed he would then have to make a
> bonfire of his canoes, his sheets of engraved
> copper and fine blankets of at least an equal
> value."

It is difficult, we are told, with our way of seeing things, "to put on one side our picture of the universe as a perpetual struggle and to see it with the eyes of the Pueblo Indians. They do not see the seasons, or human existence as a journey between life and death: life is always present, death is always present. Death is not a negation of life. The seasons unfold before us – and so does the life of man. And yet their attitude does not imply resignation, any subordination of desires to a superior form but rather a sense of profound identity between man and the universe."

Difficult, yes, but not impossible. This language is not entirely strange to us. We find in it echoes of the great mystical songs of our own past. We will of course guard against any excessive comparison. This beginning of an analogy is only valuable at one level: it shows quite simply that inner connections sometimes establish themselves between one culture and another.

The mistake would consist in wanting to isolate such and such a characteristic from the cultural whole, of which it is a part, in order to associate it with some other one which resembles it in another culture – which, unfortunately, is what many authors have done since Frazer's *The Golden Bough*. As Ruth Benedict puts it: "One ends up accordingly with a sort of mechanical Frankenstein monster whose right eye comes from Fiji, the left from Europe, one leg from the Tierra del Fuego, the other from Tahiti, the fingers and toes from yet other regions."

This brief survey will help us better to measure the breadth and complexity of the problem faced by contemporary man. Without neglecting, for all that, a deepening of his knowledge of the geographical (even regional) and historical lie of the land which determine his natural belonging to the land of his birth, he must more and more open himself to the song of the world. Because it is no longer permissible to imagine the culture of any one of our countries isolating itself artificially from the great currents which are passing through it, any more than it is possible nowadays to live within a closed economy.

There is simple evidence of this at the level of international relations: a common cultural ground has become indispensable to us as the basic condition of a system of exchange and sharing of research on the planetary scale. For this category of goods there are no frontiers, no customs. Thought circulates without visas. Truth lies on both sides of the Pyrenees. The field of learning spreads endlessly in all directions.

To this area a further dimension has been added by the work of historians and archaeologists in these last decades, the fabulous exploration of the two and a half to three thousand years preceding our own time.

And this mass of information constitutes the raw materials of a universal culture which we must sift from the growing chaos. Illusory universality, to be sure: surface mirage which can sometimes deceive us, enough to make us forget for a while our profound thirst. But to turn away from it, to ignore it, would be even more absurd. We must, as we say, "move with the times", "keep up to date", respect the rules of the game. Each one of us should strive, for his part, towards a "subjective universality" where these countless reflections would take their place. But what a wager!

In the twentieth century, Pascal's "man of honour" has a decidedly bad conscience. Too many riches assail him on all sides and he does not know how to receive them, choose among them, digest them. The famous "intellectual baggage" is more and more cumbersome. Would it not be better, "honestly", to leave it in the left luggage department until such time as we know what to do with its contents?

On the ocean of scientific discoveries we drift at the mercy of prevailing currents. The inventory of learning needs to be re-made daily and any synthesis becomes a trap. Between the deceptive charms of vulgarisation and the dangers of excessive specialisation, the situation becomes intolerable.

"To move with the times" – what does that mean? To adapt one's existence, one's desires, one's thoughts as much as possible to the new norms? But if some of these rules are asserting themselves, most of them are still in gestation: they will come from a huge brew of materials springing up from all over the place at any moment, to be sorted out, rejected, taken up again and tried out unceasingly in new combinations. Most often this will take place without you, or me, without "them", without anyone . . . anyone who could be held responsible, let alone aware of the final choice.

There will be no lack of well- (or ill-) intentioned people in the event, to predict the decline of the West or the disintegration of culture, forgetting that, as Sorokin observes so opportunely, what has never been integrated cannot be disintegrated.

It is no less true that this "integration" is proving more and more impossible. Extraversion is at its height, as our fever for the conquest of space shows, and this unlimited projection of our destiny calls forth that never-ending accelerated movement by which, in an expanding universe, each galaxy madly distances itself from its place of origin.

To return to Paul Mus again: we can say that the balance between culture and civilisation is broken and that the most salient characteristic of our time, this subordination of pure science to a programme of absolutely dizzying technical "achievements", makes it

more and more difficult to seize hold of and clarify their possible
significance. Some intrepid seekers try to, all the same and their
undertaking needs to be followed carefully: Stephane Lupasco among
others, who up to now was working in semi-obscurity, but whose
recent book, *Les trois matières* has made him known to the public at
large.

> "One of the most significant events of our
> time," he writes, "is without doubt this
> growing gap between the data of an
> increasingly audacious scientific experience
> and the mental traditions, the old forms of our
> customary logical apparatus: apparatus as
> tyrannical as it is unconscious and richer from
> the successes of the past. And, as we know,
> only by inflicting on it some painful wrenches
> could micro-physics open the field to these
> disturbing adventures with which everybody
> is familiar . . .
>
> Now, one essential point has been
> established since Einstein. If matter presents
> itself these days under three aspects –
> macro-physical (inanimate) matter, living
> matter and micro-physical matter (neither
> *animate, nor inanimate*) whose strange
> manifestations form the subject of quantum
> physics – everything, in this matter with its
> three aspects, is reduced to *energy*.
>
> It remains difficult, nevertheless, for us to
> really *believe*, to *live* practically the theoretical
> conviction that all the objects which surround
> us, including solids, such as our flesh, our
> bones even, have nothing 'material' about
> them – in the millenial and instinctive sense of
> the concept of matter – and that they are only
> (beyond what our perception and the
> powerful creations of our pragmatic
> consciousness suggest to us) the more or less
> resisting manifestations and systematisations
> of energy."

For my part I will add that *for us* nothing would be more absurd or
false. At this reckoning, if the means were offered to us, how many
light years would we need in order to explore the field of an event

which, on our plane of existence, takes place in a few seconds?

Recognition of the relativity of our palpable experience comes not by casting it out beyond reality, but, rather the opposite, by re-situating it in its right place by restoring its proper validity at the level which corresponds to it. In order to come closer to this idea of energy, Lupasco, in ascertaining that "any energy system is made up of opposing forces, depending on the nature and the mechanism even of the events of which it is constituted," outlines a new dialectic of an essentially *dynamic* nature, based on what he calls "the principle of antagonism," principle which he sums up in these words: "an energy, a dynamism, an event, whatever it may be, always implies an antagonistic energy, an antagonistic dynamism, an antagonistic event, so that the relative actualisation of one leads to the relative potentialisation of the other."

But the scope of this "logic of contradiction" would remain rather narrowly limited to a better understanding of the data of contemporary science, if Lupacso had not already invited us to have an inkling, based on the same principle, of an analogy between the psychical experience and the micro-physical experience, and to "re-think psychology at one and the same time with regard to the structure of its object, the fact submitted to its investigation and to its operative logic."

In the properly scientific domain, the practical scope of this analogy is now obvious: it has been necessary to recognise the primordial role of the thinking of the researcher and its decisive intervention not only on the conduct but on the nature and materiality of the experiment. Thus the *person* of the scholar finds its place once more at the centre of the laboratory, from whence since the 19th century it had been, as it were, exiled, along with God.

The problem will be seen to be even greater, if we are willing to admit that the psyche, "seat *par excellence* of ambivalences, tensions and contradictory tendencies, brings about, makes a reality of the unending conflict between the two systems, physical and biological, in which it equally takes part."

It is this intrinsic contradiction of the psychic phenomenon which explains, according to Lupasco, its most significant products, those which are an integral part of it: signs, symbols, concepts and myths. In any case "doesn't the thinking of so-called primitive peoples, like that of civilised peoples, create myth with the sole purpose of getting away from history and of penetrating the timeless: myth is engendered by this thinking *as an irresistible emanation of its very composition*."

As a consequence, what new perspectives on the different

domains of culture reveal themselves!

Will it be necessary for us one day to consider the systematisation proposed by Lupasco as a new *Discours de la méthode*? It is doubtless too early to affirm this: however seductive his systematisation is, it certainly needs to be studied more deeply and to be seriously tested. Moreover, don't let us forget, Hegelian dialectic, corrected or not by Marx, appeared also as a new way of thinking, implying in itself a genuine *change of being*. Who can boast of having really achieved this other than in lightning flashes?

It is true that this dialectic, inasmuch as it has acted as a *ferment*, has played a considerable role which Lupasco's suggestions could well revive in their own way, if only by maintaining in man the most fruitful dissatisfactions, the real thirst for searching. Lupasco himself already recognises the limits of his system by establishing the irreductibility of the affective data, which he describes as "a fundamental enigma" and by leaving to the mystics the experience of the "trans-psychic".

In front of this partial failure of a thinking which stops at the threshold of an experience where the emotional being would have its place, isn't it tempting to turn, as a last resort, towards *Art*? Between the world of principles where any relationship with transcendental knowledge belongs and the world of changing forms which constitutes its necessary support, is not Art the best suited way to apprehend the real, where the senses, the intellect and the feelings find once more their original unity? This is what gives Art such a power of suggestion and allows it to act on century upon century of human sensitivity and intelligence.

But Art, in its turn, cannot be conceived in isolation. In order to be more than a distraction, an amusement, a wanton game for the use of lovers of new sensations, it demands from the one who practises it a special asceticism, within the larger framework of this "art of living" which remains the great concern of every human being from the moment he becomes aware of his true destiny.

So here we are – back, by another route, at our starting point, in front of the same living and stimulating question. We have tried to envisage various aspects of this fundamentally social phenomenon which culture is, but without forgetting that being such it concerns each one of us. For if society gives form to the individuals of which it is composed, they, and some more than others, repay it richly.

Surely the increasing isolation of pioneers of research, in the domain of art as in the domain of science, is there to remind us of the great significance of the individual adventure? If the scholar, like the artist re-discovers an active place at the very centre of the experiment, each one of us, in his way, and within the limits of his possibilities, is meant to do as much in relation to his own existence.

In questioning himself about culture man re-discovers his most intimate problem: *who am I* really – and what, objectively, can be asked of me?

The only way available to me to become aware of my relationship with culture is to take an active part in it, by striving to make it my own.

But before becoming what is called a "cultured man" the individual is a waste land, sown with stones, full of brambles and scrub.

In front of his waste land the peasant asks himself: can even this earth be cultivated? Once I have cleared it, dug it over, improved it, prepared it for sowing, what am I then going to plant in it? And what harvest will I get from it? Because for the peasant there is no "art for art's sake"; no culture for culture's sake – especially when the peasant and his field are one and the same thing. "What's the point, he will say, of burying my field beneath crops if it is to find myself, at the end of the day, hopelessly the same?"

Culture is a process of transformation. To cultivate one's field is to bring about one's own metamorphosis to well-determined ends – and this is the adventure in which the whole being finds itself engaged.

The man who is in love with real culture aspires to a tranformation *of himself* through knowledge. All knowledge seems pointless to him if it is not first and foremost *self-knowledge*. For it is only inasmuch as he knows himself that he knows how to choose his nourishment according to his real needs.

And in order to be the sole master of his choice he works to free his thoughts, his feelings, his senses even, from their tyrannical routine, or rather to free himself from them by bringing about his own inner revolution, not for stupidly selfish ends, but so that his attempt to be a part of society is at last filled with meaning.

L.D. – Does the memory of your dreams have any particular influence on your behaviour (in your opinion?)

H.T. – I don't understand it very well. My daydreams have a much more evident action or effect!

I would be tempted to say "forget the 'stuff of dreams'" if I didn't feel how many secret links have united my daydreams with my nocturnal ones. It is rare, at all events, for the *direct* memory of my nocturnal life to obsess me in my waking state. My day is bathed in dreams of which I see only the surface, ostensible reason: I don't know what couplings take place in me in the depths.

"Why Sleepest Thou, O Lord?"

Awake, why sleepest thou, O Lord?
Arise, cast us not off for ever.
(Psalms 44:23)

Indeed, why does He sleep? If the Almighty cannot help sleeping, we may wonder whether it is not for some utterly binding reason – if only for the sake of conforming to the laws of His own Creation. For since the very first day, when he divided the light from the darkness, sleep has been imperative.

Without sleep, no awakening: such is the universal law of alternation which, according to ancient traditions, applies to Creation itself. In going back as far as Vedic India, we find in the Laws of Manu: "When that divine one wakes, then this world stirs; when he slumbers tranquilly, then the Universe sinks to sleep." "The Manvantaras (creation and destruction of the world) are numberless; in sport, as it were, the Creator repeats this again and again." Every time the world is suspended or resorbed, Vishnu peacefully reclines on the cosmic serpent, Ananta, which means "endless".

Why sleepest thou, O Vishnu? A fascinating vision, and so unfathomable that it leaves no room for speculation, for any attempt to reduce it to our scale. And yet endlessly in the secret heart of our own mystery, how can we not wonder?

And if all this was but a dream? When asked by a pupil, "If it is true that the world is God's dream, then what happens when God wakes up?" a Sufi master in the Near East replied: "The world is not God's dream. It is man's dream. And when man wakes, he finds there is only God. Nothing else is real truth (*haq*). The whole world is merely ripples in the Ocean of Truth. Surface stuff. *Look deeper*. Ripples arise; but it is all water, the same water, only water. To awaken is to *see* that."

Am I able to look deeper? And if not, doesn't the question become: Why do I sleep? And do I even know what sleep is?

According to the Upanishads, there are four states of being: the waking state "common to all men" (*jāgarita-sthāna*) comes first; then the dreaming state (*svapna-sthāna*); followed by the deep sleep state (*suṣupta-sthāna*); and eventually the fourth (superconscious) state (*turīya*), "with which there can be no dealing," the very Self (*Ātman*).

Reprinted by kind permission of the late D.M. Dooling, founding editor of PARABOLA magazine where it first appeared in Vol. VII, No. 1, 1981 on Sleep.

Deep sleep: what is this third state, this unknowable "deep sleep"? Is it the one God caused to fall upon Adam in order to create out of one of his ribs "an helpmeet for him"? The Māndukya Upanishad says: "If one asleep desires no desire whatsoever, sees no dream whatsoever, that is deep sleep (*suṣupta*)." The Brihad-Āranyaka Upanishad says: "As a falcon or an eagle, having flown around here in space, becomes weary, folds its wings, and is borne down to its nest, just so does this person hasten to that state where, asleep, he desires no desires and sees no dream·"

Dreamless sleep appears to be far beyond any definable concept; in the Chāndogya Upanishad it is said to be "the ultimate," the "cognitional," and to consist of bliss, eternal Bliss. "Now when one is thus sound asleep, composed, serene, and knows no dream, that is the Self (*Ātman*), that is the immortal, the fearless, that is Brahma."

So that, "having enjoyed himself in that state of deep sleep, having moved about and seen good and evil, he hastens back again as he came to the place of origin, back to sleep" (Brihad-Āranyaka).

Back to sleep as the deepest possible source of full cognition and bliss. No wonder, therefore, that so many Western as well as Eastern "seekers of truth" give it so much value as a propitious ground for their search.

Chuang Tzu wrote: "Everything is one; during sleep the soul, undistracted, is absorbed into this unity; when awake, distracted, it sees the different beings." Some fourteen centuries later, Bernard of Clairvaux praises the "*vitalis vigilque sopor*," a "sleep alive and watchful," which enlightens the inward senses. And al-Ghazzālī considered sleep the most appropriate, though remote, reflection of what is known as prophetic vision: "A blind man can understand nothing of colors save what he has learned by narration and hearsay. Yet God has brought prophetism near to men in giving them all a state analogous to it in its principal characters. This state is sleep."

We may find an echo of this in the "dark contemplation" of John of the Cross, or in the "innate spirits in man" Paracelsus speaks of ("for it is the Light of Nature which is at work during sleep") or again in Avicenna's dove (soul), which "spies such things as cannot be witnessed by waking eyes."

But here we must be on guard. For is our sleep this deep sleep of vision, and is our waking really waking?

It must be remembered, as the great masters have warned, that there are always traps and false paths in the quest for the unknown. The yearning of the mystics of all religions for another state of being – whether it is called ecstasy, enlightenment, or liberation – must be rigorously examined. These lines from Fray Francisco de Osuna (however enraptured Teresa of Avila may have been when she first read them) require a closer look:

> "Blessed are they who pray before going to
> sleep and who, on awakening, return
> promptly to prayer. Like Elias they eat a little,
> sleep, eat again a little and nestle in the arms of
> the Lord like children who fall asleep at their
> mother's breast, having drunk her milk, wake
> again, suckle and fall asleep again. Thus, with
> these glorious intervals, their time asleep
> counts as prayer more than as sleep . . . And
> although they have slept, they realize on
> awakening that their soul has slept in the arms
> of the Beloved."

These words unavoidably call to mind the *regressus ad uterum*, the yearning to return to the sleep of the maternal womb. This natural reaction has been studied by Professor A. Tomatis in his *Libération d'Oedipe*:

> "The new-born baby suddenly finds himself
> flooded in light. Confronted by this sudden
> and intense brightness, which accompanies
> the entry into the world of the big people, of
> the giants, he chooses to escape into sleep as
> the only way for him to take refuge, forgetting
> his present condition and remembering the
> past in which he lived in his previous
> existence, his foetal existence.
>   Very few men afterwards ever know how
> to disengage themselves from this grip of
> sleep, this very first refusal to face life as it is.
> The physiological limits of the state of sleep are
> often largely exceeded by an intention,
> archaically anchored, to flee the present to the
> point of not being."

This thoughtful evaluation of sleep requires further pondering, but let us once again scan the four states of being as defined in the Upanishads.

The last and highest one, the superconscious *turīya*, we shall of course keep in sight as our deeply attractive but inaccessible horizon. Closest to it is the deep and dreamless state (*suṣupta*) which we have been trying to explore. As for the dreaming state (*svapna*), we could be promptly lost in its utterly polyvalent network of lures, and so we are compelled first of all to consider the lowest one (*jāgarita*), the so-called "waking state."

Awakening gives the appearance of being a sort of victory over sleep, but what if this were only a semblance, another lure, another dream? "Life is a dream; when we sleep we are awake, and when we awake we sleep," says Montaigne. We are familiar with such notions as daydreaming and absentmindedness, but while we notice these propensities in our fellow men, we hardly ever acknowledge them in ourselves; or when we do, we take it as the exception rather than the rule.

At times, in the course of the day, I come to. As it were, I awake in a flash: "Here I am," more or less intensely. Then, without realizing it, I quickly sink back into that ambiguous state – "paradoxical waking state" we could call it (in contrast with the overused "paradoxical sleep") – in which I am neither fully awake nor fast asleep.

Unavoidably, I mistake these fleeting experiences for my normal state, as if they were going to last, whereas in fact an automatism promptly takes over and deals in a more or less acceptable way with the functional requirements of my day-to-day existence.

If I become partly aware of this bewildering situation, I may acknowledge – with a smile – that it is so and, knowingly, pretend to accept it. But of course this might be just another trap into which, unknowingly, I fall unless, prompted by an enigmatic sense of urgency, I try to stay there and look deeper.

Striving to stay there, aware of my own presence, while everything moves inside me as well as outside, my power of attention, however well trained it may be for other tasks, is at once helplessly swept away from this intimate perception by tidal waves of associations. Over and over again, I may try to take up the challenge and resume this private search for authenticity, which nobody on earth can ever undertake for me. And yet by dint of trying, failing, and trying again, I come to the point where I realize how much I am in need of help.

And help is there. Am I so blind and so deaf as to ignore it? It offers itself in many guises – testimonies of all kinds, sacred books, spiritual ways.

Take, for instance, Buddhist asceticism, the way of the Buddha towards awakening. For "Buddha," from the root *budh*, to awaken, means the "Awakened One." It is thus a designation applied to one who attains spiritual realization, likened to an "arousing" or to an "awakening." He reaches the path, as stated in the Majjhimanikaya, "by the intensity, the constancy and the concentration of the will," then "of the energy," then "of the spirit," then "of investigation," and last "of a heroic spirit." "And thus attaining these heroic qualities, he is able, O disciples, to achieve liberation, to achieve awakening."

In my own effort towards concentration, help is also offered by nature itself, life itself – whenever I can remain permeable to the deeply revealing impressions that it never ceases to provide. Therefore, my only concern should be to try and stay attentive to the wordless call from that which is always there, waiting for recognition.

Re-cognition. This might prove to be the key, not to try to "reach for," but just to come back to what is. "To remember myself," in Gurdjieff's language, means to come back to my *real* self: "Life is real only then, when *I* am." Which implies that what we call "life" is totally unreal – as well as what we call "I".

The so-called "waking state" is in the way. "A modern man lives in sleep, in sleep he is born and in sleep he dies," writes Ouspensky, quoting Gurdjieff. To awake from this sleep will be the first step toward real being and real life, for "the sleep and waking states are equally subjective. Only by beginning to remember himself does a man really awaken."

How far is it given a man to remember himself? "Theoretically he can, but practically it is almost impossible because as soon as a man awakens for a moment, all the (hypnotic) forces that caused him to fall asleep begin to act upon him with tenfold energy and he immediately falls asleep again, very often *dreaming* that he is awake, or is awakening."

This might help us find a sounder approach to the old perplexing aphorism: "A man may be born, but in order to be born he must first die, and in order to die he must first awake."

"To awake, to die, to be born," which reads now: *to awake* from this so-called "waking state"; to *die* to the misleading reactions that we usually mistake for "life"; and to be *born* again to the higher potentialities of being, evidence of the real intention behind our presence on earth.

If a man proves able to conquer his expectation of reward for his achievements, he might even come to wonder whether life has not been granted him for this very challenge: to accept and play his part in the mystery with his eyes wide open, as man alone can do, through a lifetime of "conscious labors and intentional sufferings."

Hope is there, objective hope; dormant potentialities never vanish. Hidden as they are, they bear witness to the sacred presence, the sleeping god within. And although I forget, over and over again, – why sleepest thou, O Lord? – there is a way out of this maze. A very long one indeed . . . It may take a lifetime (and perhaps even more), but it starts here and now.

Thus Spake Beelzebub

I t all began with a catastrophe.
       Due to the "erroneous calculations" of some member of the "Most High Commission of Arch-Engineers Archangels specialists in the work of World-Creation and World-Maintenance," the comet Kondoor, when crossing for the first time our solar system Ors, unexpectedly ran against the brand new planet called Earth, and they "collided so violently that from this shock . . . two large fragments were broken off from the planet Earth and flew into space."*

"Glory to Chance . . . the peaceful existence of that system Ors was soon reestablished" – but certain measures had to be taken later to palliate the menace of subsequent "irreparable calamities" on a greater cosmic scale.

It is just at this point that we human beings appear on the scene. For it seems that the chief reason for our arising on Earth, as "biped Tetartocosmoses," was to manufacture by our very existence the vibrations required for the maintenance of the two detached fragments of our planet – namely Moon and the long-forgotten "Anoulios".

Moreover, fearing that, from the realization of such a slavery to "circumstances utterly foreign to them," these bipeds would merely wish to destroy themselves, the Most High Commission once again made a big mistake by deciding to actualize a special measure, the consequences of which, "unforeseen from Above," eventually turned into a "malignant sore," not only for this ill-fated planet and its inhabitants, but for the whole Universe.

This measure consisted of implanting provisionally into the bodies of these unfortunate beings a "special organ called Kundabuffer," which made them "perceive reality topsy-turvy."

And here is our curse: although some time later, the said organ, having been proved to be no longer necessary, was actually "removed

Reprinted by permission of Triangle Editions Inc. This article first appeared in MAITREYA No. 6 on Order, Shambala (1977).

* See G.I. Gurdjieff: All and Everything, First Series, Beelzebub's Tales to His Grandson. (New York: E.P. Dutton & Co., 1964) pp. 83-89, and passim.

from their bodily presences," the consequences of its properties remained crystallized in their psyche and were fully transmitted from generation to generation down to their remote descendants – in other words, to you and me.

Among these utterly unbecoming consequences, Beelzebub tells us, were to be found such uncontrolled tendencies as: "arrogance, the need to provoke astonishment in others, bragging, cunning, the vice of eating, egoism, envy, hate, imagination, jealousy, lying, offensiveness, partiality, pride, "sandoor" or wishing the death or weakness of others, self-conceit, self-love, swagger, vanity." and so on.

What to think of it? After all, while such a jumble is in no way pleasant to inventory nor easy to digest, as far as one is concerned as an individual, one could still live in hopes of finding a way to put up with it.

But there is worse – much worse. For sooner or later these "consequences" had to meet and to blend – consequences had to breed consequences, so that the resulting tendencies began to develop and develop "like a Jericho trumpet in crescendo" into the periodic and devastating urge "to destroy the existence of others like oneself," which meant wars on an ever-increasing scale, to the point of jeopardizing the whole human species.

This is our first approach to Gurdjieff's ideas, as they are expressed in the initial (and monumental) series of his writings: a dreadful, apocalyptic vision of man's fate in relation to the Universe, man's deep and persistent delusions, man's increasing loss of control, man's delirious propensity towards self-extermination. His lot is *disorder*, again disorder, more and more disorder.

Distressing perspective if ever there was one: all our beliefs in human capacities for endless progress, all our anticipation of a better world encounter here a blunt denial.

But had we not been warned? Did not Gurdjieff designate his "Beelzebub's Tales" as "an objectively impartial criticism of the life of man," in which his ostensible purpose was "to destroy, mercilessly, in the mentation and feelings of the reader, the beliefs and views, by centuries rooted in him, about everything existing in the world"?

So that from now on, it is up to us. We may refuse to go further – turn our back on this haunting vision and try to forget about it. After all, this is not the first time that, on the verge of disclosing the truth of man's real situation, prophets caution their listeners against mere curiosity: "Beware! This is not soft drink! – if you are not dying of thirst, you had better forbear . . . "

Now, are we that thirsty? Really able to swallow it? We are then forewarned of a new danger: "Don't be gullible. Watch carefully. Do not take anything for granted: wait until you have seen it for yourself. And this may take time, much time – a lifetime perhaps."

Are we that patient? Nowadays everything is prompting us to hurry. Acceleration rules all our functions, if we want to keep up. Indeed to try and be patient definitely goes against the grain.

Are we ready? Are we fully aware of our situation, and bold enough to try?

It sounds like a challenge.

Are we merely to accept Beelzebub's cosmogony as gospel?

But, first of all, who is Beelzebub, according to Gurdjieff?

The Hebrew Lord of the Flies? One of Satan's lieutenants? A partner of "Arch-cunning Lucifer"?

Nothing of the kind.

When he was young, "owing to his extraordinary resourceful intelligence," Beelzebub had been "taken into service on the Sun Absolute" – the most central part of our great Universe – "as an attendant upon His Endlessness." And not only had he nothing in common with the Chaos principle, but he was a most eager defender of Order.

So eager, that having seen "in the government of the World something which seemed to him "illogical," and having found support among his comrades, he interfered in what was none of his business" with such impetuosity that he brought "the central kingdom of the Megalocosmos almost to the verge of revolution."

As a result, he was banished with all his followers to a very remote corner of the world – namely to our system Ors – where he spent many "years," according to an objective calculation of time (in other words, a good many of our centuries), in sincere repentance of his fault – until the All-Merciful, on account of his invaluable services, granted him His forgiveness and called him back from exile.

Let us admit it: does this story not ring a secret bell in us?

Even if it does not fit in with our previous ideas about the demonic figure, it does evoke something more than the usual prejudices: an impression of tacit understanding and even of respect for his attitude, as if we felt at one with him, first in his sincere indignation and his immature but imperative wish to serve what he regarded as more right, then in his honesty to own up to his guilt, and in his full acceptance to atone for it.

"Errors of youth," we may think. But now that he is such a fully experienced veteran, are we not ready to sit beside his grandson

Hassein and listen to him with a more genuine interest?

Grandfather Beelzebub speaks, and his tone of voice sounds so natural, so convincing, that we might merely fall under its spell and forget all our previous circumspection.

But the old narrator is on the watch, as if he were staring at us and observing our slightest reaction, and he takes corresponding measures until at times we can't help noticing some overstatement, or some deliberate insinuation, too obvious to be ignored, for example, when he calls our attention to the "excessive elevation" of the Tibetan peaks, which causes the atmosphere of the planet Earth to acquire in its turn an "excessively projecting materialized presence," so that at certain times it "hooks on, as it were, to the atmosphere of other planets or comets" and eventually originates threatening tremors or quakes . . . And this rings like a discreet alarm, by which he reminds us to keep awake – for credulity, as he says, is unworthy of man.

On the other hand, we may catch more subtle vibrations here and there, in amongst his winding sentences, inviting us to discover some further meaning underneath, without which we would miss the essential.

Yes. For in spite of the author's "friendly advice" to skim through these tales "as you have already become mechanized to read all your contemporary books and newspapers" – which, by the way, is simply unfeasible – there is sufficient evidence that from the very beginning he also expects us to look for a better approach to Beelzebub's intimations, until we are able to "try and fathom the gist" of his message.

Will this help us to overcome our first impression from this account of general failure, of perpetual tumbling from disaster to disaster, of provisional and manifestly inadequate or insufficient attempts at redeeming the successive errors?

First of all, let us remember that in more than one ancient myth we are confronted with a very similar situation: at the very beginning something is missing, something does not correspond, something goes wrong. The first-born is a cripple, dwarf or Cyclops, a kind of monster that has to be slaughtered or metamorphosed, and so on and so forth.

There seems to be a doom on the very creation. Does not the great Demiurge endanger the mysterious Order that prevailed beforehand? The slightest change in the perfect Unity of the pre-existent Harmony is apt to engender all sorts of perturbations for which endless measures of compensation have to be found. Such is the unknowable riddle of that which is neither manifested nor "non-manifested," and which transcends the unavoidable contradiction between the principle and whatever its form of actualization.

But in *Beelzebub's Tales*, we deal only with the stage preceding the outer creation, when our Uni-Being and Omnipotent Creator found Himself suddenly confronted with the slow but undeniable action of the merciless Heropass, that is, the flow of Time.

His Endlessness then "devoted Himself entirely to finding a possibility of averting such an inevitable end . . . and after His long Divine deliberations, He decided to create our present existing "Megalocosmos."

As a result, He was compelled to alter accordingly "the system of functionings of the two fundamental cosmic laws, called the sacred Heptaparaparshinokh (Law of Seven) and the sacred Triamazikamno (Law of Three)."

Now let us prick up our ears! For at this very point in his narrative, Beelzebub gives his grandson invaluable advice, which could prove to be of tremendous significance for us, inasmuch as we are able to decipher it, to take it in, and to put it into practice:

"I repeat, my boy: try very hard to understand everything that will relate to both these fundamental cosmic sacred laws, since . . . an all-round awareness of everything concerning these sacred laws conduces in general to this, that three-brained beings . . . , by becoming capable, in the presence of all cosmic factors not depending on them and arising round about them – both the personally favorable as well as the unfavorable – of pondering on the sense of existence, acquire data for the elucidation and reconciliation in themselves of what is called "individual collision" which often arises, in general, in three-brained beings from the contradiction between the concrete results flowing from the processes of all cosmic laws and the results presupposed and even quite surely expected by their what is called "sane logic"; and thus, *correctly evaluating the essential significance of their own presence*, they become aware of the genuine corresponding place for themselves in these common-cosmic actualizations."

Well . . . once again we may find ourselves at a loss. It would probably take a lifetime to elucidate the real content of such phrases as Heptaparaparshinokh and Triamazikamno, in their unknown technicality.

Meanwhile, we shall keep in mind that, according to Beelzebub, we, as contemporary human "three-brained beings" able to think, to sense and move, and to feel, are still endowed with all the possibilities to assimilate and transform, from the cosmic substances that we absorb, the necessary elements "for the coating and for the perfecting of higher-being-bodies" in ourselves – that is, for the reanimation of such dormant potentialities that are meant to enable us to come closer to our real destination.

Thus, some objective hope is left to us: our doom is neither total nor final.

As a matter of fact, it was just to foster this revival and provide an actual support for these given possibilities that in 1922 Gurdjieff founded his "Institute for the Harmonious Development of Man" at the Prieuré d'Avon, near Fontainebleau. There, he made a point of preventing those who came to him, and who were already out of their teens, from falling into "the usual pessimism everywhere prevalent in the contemporary abnormal life," assuring them that "even for you, it is not yet too late."

It is not too late to try and restore the forgotten order to which our remote ancestors belonged, before the consequences of the properties of this accursed organ Kundabuffer were completely crystallized in our tyrannical associative system.

"In everything under the care of Mother Nature," he maintains, "the possibility is foreseen for beings to acquire the kernel of their essence, that is to say, their own I."

"Not yet too late," perhaps – but not too easy, for sure.

Is not the leitmotiv of *Beelzebub's Tales* a constant call for "conscious efforts and intentional sufferings"?

Let us listen to what the author says in the concluding chapter of this First Series:

"Man – how mighty it sounds! The very name "man" means "the acme of Creation"; but . . . how does this title fit contemporary man?

"To possess the right to the name of "man" one must be one.

"And to be such, one must first of all, with an indefatigable persistence and an unquenchable impulse of desire, issuing from all the separate independent parts constituting one's entire common presence, that is to say, with a desire issuing simultaneously from thought, feeling, and organic instinct, work on an all-round knowledge of oneself – at the same time struggling increasingly with one's subjective weaknesses – and then afterwards, taking one's stand upon the results thus obtained by one's consciousness alone, concerning the defects in one's established subjectivity as well as the elucidated means for the possibility of combatting them, strive for their eradication without mercy towards oneself."

For a sounder understanding of this rather austere program, we need to realize that the second part of it is not at all an end in itself: "striving for the eradication" of our defects should not naïvely be taken in terms of "reclaiming" or "rehabilitation" in terms of mending our ways or seeking reassurance through aping any ideal pattern.

In fact, our real purpose should remain, from end to end, to *know ourselves as we are*, and this is what demands imperatively our constant struggling against our weaknesses, since all our ordinary manifestations are under the sway of suggestions that make us "reflect reality upside down," for the sake of supporting and perpetuating our self-complacency.

Now, to "work on an all-round knowledge" of ourselves means initially to make full acquaintance with the mechanicality which governs the entire network of our functionings.

And this, in turn, "is possible only as a result of correctly conducted self-observation," which implies the conscious mobilization and active cooperation of all our centres of perception and manifestation.** How much of ourselves, organically and emotionally, as well as intellectually must be engaged in this endeavour, we may surmise when we read that for a real study and experience of himself "a man must decide, once and forever, that he will be sincere with himself unconditionally, will shut his eyes to nothing, shun no results wherever they may lead him, be afraid of no inferences, and be limited by no previous, self-imposed limits," and he must be warned that to accept the inferences of such a self-observation and not lose heart he "must have great courage."

As a matter of fact, "these inferences may "upset" all the convictions and beliefs previously deep-rooted in a man, as well as the whole order of his ordinary mentation; and, in that event, he might be robbed, perhaps forever, of all pleasant, as is said, "values dear to his heart" which have hitherto made up his calm and serene life."

Is this not the reason why so many people who at first seem to be so keen on treading the arduous path of the ageless "know thyself" so quickly relinquish it? And yet . . .

"Such is the ordinary average man – an unconscious slave entirely at the service of all-universal purposes, which are alien to his own personal individuality.

** cf. *"Views from the Real World"* in *Early Talks of Gurdjieff as Recollected by His Pupils* (New York: E.P. Dutton & Co., 1973) p. 222: "Working on oneself is not so difficult as wishing to work, taking the decision. This is because our centres have to agree among themselves, having realized that, if they are to do anything together, they have to submit to a common master. But it is difficult for them to agree because once there is a master, it will no longer be possible for any of them to order the others about and to do what they like. There is no master in ordinary man . . ."

"He may live through all his years as he is, and as such be destroyed for ever.

"But at the same time Great Nature has given him the possibility of being not merely a blind tool entirely at the service of these all-universal objective purposes but, while serving Her and actualizing what is fore-ordained for him – which is the lot of every breathing creature – of working at the same time also for himself" – for his own individuality.

"This possibility was given also for service to the common purpose, owing to the fact that, for the equilibrium of these objective laws, such relatively liberated people are necessary."

There comes the miracle without which no real transformation could ever materialize.

For one who "works on an all-round knowledge of himself," if he is ready to "shun no results wherever they may lead him," there comes the moment of truth. At the very instant he awakes and sees his situation for what it is – that is, objectively, almost desperate – a *reversal* takes place: instead of giving up the struggle, with his eyes wide open he accepts the challenge. He stands up as a "man" and feels ready to try his utmost – because that is where he finds his genuine "raison d'être."

And while acknowledging quite clearly that he cannot dream of moving, thinking and deciding anything by himself he tries all the same, and *in the trying* he realizes that ultimately something is still up to him – and to him alone. For "man is a being who can do, and "to do" means to act consciously and by one's initiative."

Truly, whether he wishes it or not he is bound to submit to demands "utterly foreign to him." But the ultimate choice is left to him: rather than passively undergoing the tyranny of forces that rule all his reactions, he accepts *knowingly* to play the game for the sake of serving, through them and with their help, a higher and meaningful purpose – thus restoring in himself the underlying order to which he belongs.

For this order is in no way an outer projection, but is the living reality of which he is the bearer, even though most of the time it has been – and still is – ignored, denied or betrayed.

To restore order means to liberate oneself from the spell of what *seems*, and to come back to what *is*. To this purpose, our tendency to lie and to dream, our passive imagination, our addiction to "what is not" and our fear of "what is," have to be conquered. Instead of yielding to our familiar phantasmagoria, we shall oppose it and free ourselves from it, thereby releasing anew the intimate flow of energy which corresponds to our deeper, essential nature.

We may believe that we understand this idea, but as a rule, we do not: we promptly reduce it to the nostalgia for a "lost order" – whereas it is *we* who are lost, not order itself.

As a matter of fact, what we actually mean by "order" is necessarily limited, since it merely answers our craving for limits. And indeed, on the level of our daily existence, it fulfills perfectly its role of withstanding the constant threat of meaningless disorder. But there are other levels as well, other needs to be met, other menaces to be faced: against Chaos itself, against the Unknown, there is no safeguard. Sooner or later we shall have to relinquish our hope of feeling secure: we shall have to take our own risk.

If we really wish to persevere in our search for truth and not be satisfied with any provisional shelter, it is high time to enlarge our scope and think in terms of universal harmony, which, according to Beelzebub, depends on the "mutual influence and reciprocal maintenance of everything existing," and implies essentially – in keeping with the principle of the Law of Three – a *reconciliation of opposites*.

In other words, ultimately, this underlying Order must, in that sense, absorb, include and eventually assimilate all particular orders *and* disorders.

Now, in coming back to the imperative necessity for a man to disentangle himself from the network of countless suggestions and forms of mechanical functionings that keep him from being what he *is*, we may begin to understand why this renouncement, this "death" to all our "automatically and slavishly acquired habits" is the only key to a new way of life.

Thus the Gospel parable: "Except a corn of wheat fall into the ground and die, it abideth alone; but, if it die, it bringeth forth much fruit."

To which Gurdjieff echoes by another aphorism: "A man may be born, but in order to be born he must die, and in order to die he must first awake."***

"It is just this death that is spoken of in all religions.

"It is defined in the saying which has reached us from remote antiquity, "without death no resurrection," that is to say "if you do not die you will not be resurrected."

"The death referred to is not the death of the body, since for such

---

*** P.D. Ouspensky: *In Search of the Miraculous*. (London: Routledge & Kegan Paul, 1950) (New York: Harcourt Brace & Jovanovich, 1950) p. 217.

a death there is no need of resurrection.

"For if there is a soul, and moreover, an immortal soul, it can dispense with a resurrection of the body.

"No! Even Jesus Christ and all the other prophets sent from Above spoke of the death which might occur even during life, that is to say, of the death of that "Tyrant" from whom proceeds our slavery in this life and whose destruction can alone assure the first chief liberation of man·"****

But, strangely enough, our striving for this inner "death" is most effectively impeded by our basic incapacity, or reluctance, to envisage for any length of time the unavoidable prospect of our own physical death – apparently for fear of losing all interest in whatever is meant to stir us up to action.

According to Gurdjieff, this incapacity corresponds to an objective measure of protection, for in the present conditions of existence the average man "cannot and *must not* look his own death in the face." The ground would give way under his feet and before him, in clear-cut form, the question would arise: "Why should we live and toil and suffer?" And he would merely wish to hang himself.

"Precisely that such a question may not arise, Great Nature . . . was constrained to adapt Herself to such an abnormality" and to take all appropriate steps.

Nevertheless, in so far as he sincerely craves for Truth, fearlessly awakes to his situation and realises his helplessness and nothingness, as long as he is reduced to his chimerical independence, the searcher may become worthy of opening to an impartial vision of his proper destiny as a "man," a lawfully conscious reflection of the universal order."

Are we becoming too presumptious? Indeed it may seem to us that we are now equal to putting ourselves in the position of such a high cosmic realization as Mr. Beelzebub himself – and this of course without ever losing an objective sense of proportion, nor the sense of humor which, by the way, he never parts with, even in his most bitter appreciation of the catastrophic "unforeseeingness" of our Most Saintly Cosmic Individuals, experts in the work of World-Creation and World-Maintenance . . .

That is why, without relinquishing in the least our objective birthright to play our part now in the common attempt at the endless restoring of order, we may understand our impartial guide when, in answering his grandson's question, he offers as his "last vow" to His

---

**** G.I. Gurdjieff: *Beelzebub's Tales. pp. 1232 – 1233.*

Endlessness this ultimate solution:

"Thou All and the Allness of my Wholeness!

"The sole means now for the saving of the beings of the planet Earth would be to implant again into their presences a new organ, an organ like Kundabuffer, but this time of such properties that everyone of these unfortunates during the process of existence should constantly sense and be cognizant of the inevitability of his own death as well as of the death of everyone upon whom his eyes or attention rests."

May the All-Mighty hear this call! So that the remote descendants of our great-grandchildren may find, thanks to this most daring operation, more proper conditions for the fulfillment of their "Partkdolg-duties."

But as for ourselves . . .

Should we wait?

L.D. – Describe Mr Gurdjieff.

H.T. – At the outset I would perhaps have said to you: he's a bit like Dr Rabelais. Toady I am tempted to reply: Mr Gurdjieff? I don't know him!

This seemingly crazy old man – truth falls from his lips as from a child's sometimes. This peasant from the Danube with the guile of a Chinese diplomat. A real goodness, ill-concealed by his rages. A contained, a restrained violence gives his slightest kindness a disturbing flavour.

Who is he, then, behind these masks? And yet, through the ensemble of characters he acts out for us, we feel the strength of his unity, his oneness – but that, of course, is indescribable.

Testimony

Arnaud Desjardins – I spent twelve or thirteen years of my life as a member of what are called "the Gurdjieff groups," and I would like to ask our guest, Henri Tracol, to clarify for us the place of P.D. Ouspensky's book on Gurdjieff's teaching; first of all, the reason for its title: *Fragments of an Unknown Teaching*. Fragments?

Henri Tracol – Yes, why this title? It seems there couldn't be a better one, since all testimony on an approach to truth is necessarily fragmentary. People in a hurry demand a quick synthesis, a whole life of search condensed into three pages, or ten minutes on television, and by this very demand any possible understanding is prevented.

A.D. – Time is necessary?

H.T. – Time is necessary, exactly. But what is this book, *Fragments of an Unknown Teaching*? It is the narrative of a long experience, eight years which Ouspensky spent with his teacher Gurdjieff. Of course, Gurdjieff was not at all similar to the ordinary kind of teacher, and had nothing in common with the typical schoolteacher; one might say he was the opposite. He was a teacher of search, whose function was to train seekers. For him, to be and to know were one and the same. It could be said that his doctrine and his method combined to serve a practical achievement; practical, of course, in the sense of practice, a spiritual practice that changes everything. I mean to say that his purpose was not at all to accumulate knowledge, not even to reach the highest knowledge, just for its own sake, but rather to awaken to the meaning of search. This teaching is primarily a sort of seed planting that looks toward a new birth, the birth of real being, where indeed to be and to know are one and the same.

A.D. – And was there, as it were, some sort of doorway? If we are to describe this teaching in a way that would not be just theoretical but would give some real idea of it, isn't there some kind of key, a first clue that you could give us to open a way in?

H.T. – There is a key to Gurdjieff's teaching, an extremely simple one, perhaps too simple to be immediately understood. Maybe we

Contribution to the Arnaud Desjardins programme on French television, January 1969, translated by the late D.M. Dooling.

will come back to it shortly if we try once more to understand better the reason for this title of Fragments, and why this is the most legitimate approach for someone wishing to bear witness to his experience with Gurdjieff. Ouspensky wanted to lead his reader to an experience analogous with his own, to an understanding coming from an inner bonding. He wished his reader to play with these Fragments, to let them answer one another, complete each other, and finally take part in a veritable dance of knowledge. But perhaps that demands something more than simple curiosity; it requires a very strong desire, which allows the person who approaches the truth to engage himself as totally as possible in this quest.

For instance, we might take one of the principal ideas of this teaching – the idea of sleep. Gurdjieff doesn't hesitate to represent the human being as entirely submerged in sleep; not only physical sleep at night but during the whole day; he lives in a kind of hypnotic sleep, a kind of lethargy mixed with dreams and under the sway of the all-powerful imagination.

That is an interesting idea, isn't it? Even a shocking one. It's an idea that one will accept or refuse, which will immediately evoke a whole series of suggestions and associations, which will call forth all sorts of objections, and it remains interesting. But if for once we would try to realize it as a fact, to really live it among ourselves, what would it become?

A.D. – For instance?

H.T. – For instance, there are three of us here in this studio. Are we ready to accept that we are deeply asleep, can we perceive in ourselves what this sleep is, can we entertain the idea that here we are, looking at each other, talking to each other, listening to each other, like somnambulists, in full view of thousands of equally somnambulistic television watchers? Perhaps that seems rather comic, but after all, it may be true; and if I try, with an effort to open myself, to let this evidence go deeper in me, then perhaps at a given moment I will begin to experience myself in this sleep, and that means to put myself at a certain distance from it, so that in a sense I will awake to this sleep.

A.D. – I experience the sleep?

H.T. – I *experience* this sleep.

A.D. – But I want to ask you, since our time is limited, when did you know Mr. Gurdjieff?

H.T. – My first meeting with him was in October, 1940, in Paris, and curiously, this reminds me of something you said, Arnaud Desjardins, a sudden reflection in your tales of search for the ashram in your book *Ashram*: "How many doors opening on what I was looking for have I passed by without knowing . . ." Once, Gurdjieff's door was opened to us; the question was there. The door opens, a man greets us – a Man. If it were not for his eye on us, we would be more lost than ever in this unknown world which he invites us to explore, and in which we grope and find a door, another door, more doors, often without knowing what very simple question to ask, how to be, how to knock so that the door will open to us.

A.D. – The question is renewed at every moment?

H.T. – The question is renewed at every moment. Far from being achieved, the quest *begins* with the opening of a door, and perhaps begins for good and all – that is, forever.

A.D. – What is the nature, the real nature, of this search? There are all kinds of quests; every human being, after all, is looking for something.

H.T. – Yes; this search is the eternal search which at the same time is immediate and of today. It is man's vocation to seek to know himself in order to be really what he is, but this can only be understood in a quite different perspective of time from the habitual one. This search cannot be directed toward the future nor turned mechanically to the past; it is now, at once, it is immediate or it doesn't exist. This is where we very often go wrong; we are still enslaved by certain hopes, and Gurdjieff makes short work of these hopes. There is no room for complacency in the way he offers us; he can well say that this teaching is for those who have searched and been burned, and are quite ready to be burned again.

A.D. – All this has been brought together in a book; and to conclude, I would wish that you would tell us what can be acquired from this book where so many things are said and set forth.

H.T. – Yes. It is called *Beelzebub's Tales to His Grandson*. We can say in a few words that Beelzebub is a fallen angel who has reinstated himself, and that he has a twelve-year-old grandson named Hassein; but I think that what places the book's content in a better way is an anecdote which comes from the time before it was published, when we read aloud, in the author's presence, passages from the rough draft of the French translation. One day one of us said that he found it extremely difficult to follow this unfamiliar terminology and that a barrier of rational and rationalizing demands presented itself constantly; so the question arose: How to listen to Beelzebub? Mr. Gurdjieff smiled and answered, "As Hassein listens to his grandfather."

Gurdjieff and the Science of Being

I t is said, in the East, that when a deeply spiritual man dies, it is sometimes difficult, in the beginning, to know who were his closest disciples, for they are saying to themselves: "Who, now, would dare claim to be his disciple?" However, a little later, they make themselves known, since they come to think: "Who would dare shirk from bearing witness?"

Tonight, we are going to speak about George Ivanovitch Gurdjieff. It is now more than nine years since he left us, and you see: I still hesitate to talk about him.

I had the privilege of being close to him for ten years, and I can say that *he* knew me well, without any doubt better than I knew myself. On the other hand, I am still under the impression that for my part I did not know him – or only slightly.

Who was Gurdjieff?

A writer? Surely not. He had neither the kind of culture nor the literary training which we consider indispensable for being able to write books. Nevertheless, he left us a *magnum opus*, the scope and significance of which we can as yet have only an inkling. He had something to say and he said it, in an inimitable way.

Nor was he a "philosopher". He did not use the conventional jargon of the circles who indulge themselves in highfaluting speculation. He did not "cook up" any new theory to delight the connoisseurs. Yet, in spite of his apparent lack of qualifications, this "seeker of truth" knew the way to the hidden spring from which perennial wisdom flows, and with the strong force of his determination and his conscious ability to adapt, he succeeded in giving his thought a form which allowed him to explain and transmit to the modern world the fundamental principles of an objective knowledge.

He had no other purpose than to say yet again that which had been said from the beginning of time – but to say it in a manner which arouses the desire to try it and experience it, instead of escaping into philosophical wiseacering.

This idea of knowledge as something which one must test and

(Lecture given in Spanish in 1959 at the Casa del Arquitecto, Mexico City)

taste by direct experience, puts it at loggerheads with the scientific viewpoint, inherited from the last century, which despite very important exceptions, still prevails among the majority of contemporary scholars, who are so preoccupied with placing themselves "humbly" outside the object of their investigations, thereby eliminating the "personal factor", while at the same time claiming to tame the forces of nature and to subdue even the furthest planets of our solar system.

Here then is the stumbling block. We trip over it every time we claim to know some thing from the outside, as if it really did not concern us at all.

We have forgotten the taste of real knowledge, of wisdom. Our knowledge has no longer any taste. Not from lack of interest, but our interest is drawn more and more to the periphery, and to the most spectacular results of seeming power.

By driving God from our laboratories, we were running the risk of losing the real purpose of searching, and since nothing can be undertaken without some semblance of meaning, modern savants have given their allegiance to the artificial religion of endless progress, the god of which can only be man himself, albeit an isolated man destroyed by his illusion of being alone in a universe whose life he denies.

As for those who give themselves up to the consuming passion of pure science, of "science for science's sake", they fall into the same trap as those who give themselves up to "art for art's sake": they deceive themselves and get lost in an illusion from which they can no longer escape.

It is probably these to whom Fritjof Schuon alludes, when he writes "modern man collects keys without bothering to ask if they can open doors".

It is to this greedy science, intoxicated by its apparent success, to this science which increasingly distances man from himself, that astonishingly enough, the biblical proverb applies: "The fool takes food from the dish, but forgets to put it into his mouth."

And in fact it is not the endless accumulation of new facts or of original viewpoints which should matter to us, but the possibility of integrating them, so as to enrich substantially the results.

We need to understand where this thirst for knowledge comes from and who will reap the benefit. Montaigne said: "Knowledge without conscience is the ruin of the soul". If one does not know where knowledge starts from and where it is going to, it loses its roots and goes adrift.

The harvest of discoveries falls into a bottomless pit, or else man carries it as an increasingly heavy load on his tired shoulders, without its giving him any real satisfaction.

And now if I ask myself: "Do I know myself? Am I conscious of myself?" and if I try to be sincere, the reply can only be negative. How strange it is! I exist and yet I don't know who I really am. My own life is that of a stranger I know nothing about! This time, I really feel myself at stake, and already the desire to know myself arises in me. I wish to stop being absent from my life, to discover what impedes me from being what I could be, and to bring out the potentialities which I suspect are hidden in me.

What does Gurdjieff have to say about this? He says that it is pointless to talk about knowledge, without taking into account the being to whom this knowledge refers. He also says that knowledge of oneself depends very closely on one's being – in other words, that the value and quality, if not the amount of my knowledge, correspond to what I am now. He says that if I want to develop myself, my being and my knowledge should grow "simultaneously and in a parallel direction by mutually helping one another", and from their close conjunction, understanding will emerge, that is to say, genuine *knowledge of being*.

However, Gurdjieff adds that I cannot understand this language and that each of these words can give rise to a misunderstanding on my part, as I do not have the key which would allow me to establish at each instant the point of view from which he speaks, and its exact relationship to the whole. This key exists: it is the *principle of relativity*.

According to this principle, every entity in the Universe exists only in relation to the whole to which it belongs – that is, essentially, to the extent of its participation in the Whole, and Gurdjieff gives us a vast panorama of the Universe, as being composed of worlds contained one within the other, in which we live simultaneously, and with which we are related differently.

Unfortunately, in this immensity, I feel even more lost. What is my place, what is my role, what then justifies my presence in the Universe? I see clearly that I will never resolve this enigma by myself.

What I lack is a totally new way of approaching my problem – not from outside, but from within. What I lack is a science based on direct experiences – what I lack is a science of being.

No, Gurdjieff was not a philosopher, nor a modern savant. Neither was he an erudite professor, invited to give lectures in his speciality. Nothing like that. Gurdjieff was a *master*.

I already hear the concert of protests, even though they are muted. One has heard a lot about the uselessness or the harmfulness of "masters", an idea to which we often subscribe willingly. Because the best is always so close to the worst . . . There is master and master.

Let us say that the traditional conception of the function of master is not limited to the transmission of doctrines, but signifies, rather, a true *embodiment of knowledge*, thanks to which the master can exert an effective influence in order to help the disciple in his search.

And indeed, that poses a danger, the danger of abusive interference, the danger of suggestions and of usurpations! That's what Gurdjieff calls "black magic", against which he warns us insistently: he said that its most constant characteristic is the tendency to foster passion in people, and to use them, even with the best intentions, without their knowing that they are being used, and without their *understanding* the nature of the aim proposed; he says that it comes about from "fostering credulity in people" or else "working on them through fear".

Gurdjieff, on the contrary, insists on the fact that we should do nothing without understanding what we are doing. *Understanding is the first requirement of his teaching*.

"On this way, it is not necessary to have faith", he said, "What is needed is a little trust, and not even for too long, because the sooner a man starts to put to the test the truth of what he hears, the better it is for him . . . ". Man should try out by himself the truth of what he is taught.

The science of being is not given for nothing. It costs a lot, and in the market place of real values, the only currency is conscious effort.

Here again is an idea which is not to everyone's taste. In the same way as some would do without the help of a master, there are others who deny the use of working on oneself. We read in *Fragments from an Unknown Teaching*, by Ouspensky, that "certain theories affirm that a man can receive knowledge freely, without effort on his part . . . that Higher Knowledge can be acquired *even while one sleeps."*

Nevertheless, we should beware here of a frequent misunderstanding. We are not talking here of efforts of a "forcing nature", but of the very opposite. We are talking of efforts to free oneself from useless tensions, to free oneself from the tyranny of automatic associations, to protect one's attention from the unfettered crowd of suggestions which batter us at every moment. Unfortunately, it is this kind of effort which we are always trying to avoid. We prefer to guard jealously our comfortable inner passivity, even if it means an enormous waste of energy.

This necessity for an active participation by the pupil is

underlined more clearly still when Gurdjieff adds: "There is no such thing as, nor can there be any external initiation. In reality, there can only be one's personal initiation . . . Inner growth, *change of being*, depend wholly and entirely on the work which a man does on himself . . . No one can accomplish for him the task that he himself must undertake. The only thing that another can give him, is the impulse to work . . . "

For the same reason, Gurdjieff underlines that among all aims, the most sensible is the one that relates to the desire *to be master of oneself*, because without that, nothing is possible and every other aim becomes a childish dream. To be master of oneself, that is to say, *to be one's own master*, in such a way that a master is no longer necessary.

But what a long path it is! It is clear that I shall never be master of myself for as long as I do not know myself.

In order to know myself, direct investigation is needed. I am in search of my possible form. It is a must for every natural entity, when it passes from chaos to existence, from the indeterminate to the discovery of its own structure. It would be senseless here to trust chance or to grope about in the dark: a method is necessary. This method is called "self-observation". Not the observation of my behaviour, but the observation of myself in relation to the different aspects of my functioning.

Unfortunately, as soon as I try to observe myself, I see only too well that I cannot. Something stops me. My attention is not available for so subtle a task. This is because I am totally in the power of the automatic, mental, emotional and physiological reflexes, which are already fixed in me.

"Man is a very complex machine", says Gurdjieff, a wonderful puppet, perfectly regulated, and whose outer and inner movements depend at each moment, on the influences which hold sway over his existence. "Man cannot 'do'; in him everything happens, everything 'does' itself of its own accord: his principal characteristic is the *lack of unity* in himself; and furthermore not even the slightest trace of those attributes he believes he possesses: "lucid consciousness", "free will", "permanent 'I'", "ability to do", is available to him. It may surprise you if I say that the chief feature of contemporary man is *sleep*; contemporary man never stops sleeping. And this characteristic alone is sufficient to explain all that is lacking in him".

"Contemporary man is born asleep, lives asleep and dies asleep. And what *knowledge* could a sleeping man have? If you think about it and at the same time remember that sleep is the chief feature of our being, you will soon understand that if man wishes to obtain knowledge, he should first of all think about *how to awaken himself*, that is about *how to change* his being."

There is not, nor could there be a more urgent aim for me than to awaken myself. The worst of it is that in my sleep, I am not even aware of my own presence. The whole day long I forget myself. I exist as if I were someone else. I have to make a special effort to *remember myself*.

To remember myself: that really is the linch-pin of the method. And to start with, this coincides with the act of waking up.

Now, if I understand that conscious awakening is the unique loophole through which it is possible for me to escape from the prison of my automatism, and if at the same time I recognise my present incapacity to awaken myself at will, I begin to understand that one cannot just wake up simply because one wants to.

"He who wants to wake up", says Gurdjieff, "should find other people who, like himself, are also interested in the possibility of waking up, in order to work with them. If they all agree that the first one of them to wake up, will awaken the others, they already have a chance. However, even that is not sufficient, because they can all go to sleep at the same time, and dream that they are waking up. It is therefore not enough. Still more is necessary. They must be looked after by a man who is not asleep or who does not fall asleep as easily as they do. They must find such a man to wake them up and not let them fall asleep again".

Once more, we come face to face with the imperative necessity of having a master. From this new point of view, we can say that his role will be *to create the desired conditions* – the first of them being, of course, his own presence and all that this means – so that his disciples wake up, remember themselves and remain vigilant.

This *creation of conditions* is precisely the task which the great Saint Ashiata Shiemash, the prototype of master-awakeners imposes on himself in the legendary *Tales of Beelzebub to His Grandson* by Gurdjieff, in order to allow the appearance "in the ordinary consciousness of men, of the being impulse of objective conscience, the data (or potential elements) of which remain intact in their subconscious".

Such conditions necessarily present many aspects, and should continually adapt themselves to the circumstances of the disciples, in order to meet the necessary objectives of their spiritual development. In his teaching, Gurdjieff used every means which appeared opportune to him, according to the degree of understanding of his pupils. There was a time for theoretical studies, a time for experimentations, for verifications, so that each one could put his own understanding to the test, in life conditions.

One of the props which he used a great deal was the study of the laws of manifestation, by means of movements and dances. It was not so much the external form of these movements which mattered to him, but their power of animation, to which the participants bore witness by their degree of conscious presence at the heart of the experience.

To keep alive the essential ideas of his teaching demanded of him, beyond doubt, something quite other than an abstract, rigid and dry knowledge. Here lies the secret of Gurdjieff and his astonishing capacity to use his "subjective particularities" to serve his aims.

At this level, the science of being is already an art, but an art which is essentially practical: its discovery and its practice naturally call to mind the medieval craftsmen and the initiations, both spiritual and practical, of the cathedral builders' guilds.

As we have to end, let us say that the science of being which Gurdjieff tried to share with us, can only be learnt by the direct experience, constantly renewed, of awakening to our own presence in the world, and to ourselves – with all that that implies.

At the end of the talk, the audience was invited to ask a few questions:

Q. – Gurdjieff speaks of the "essential nature" of being. What does that mean?

A. – We can say it very simply: in reality *I am*. But I don't know it . . .

It is not something that I have to invent, it's what is. But to discover that I am, I must awaken myself.

Q. – Why should I try to get closer to it?

A. – If it is that which is the truest, if it is like the centre of my own presence in the world, I can't help feeling the need to know it. I can't ignore the call. This cannot fail to remind us of "Know yourself, and you will know the Universe and its laws", the great "principle of analogy" to which Gurdjieff referred when he spoke about the exact likeness between microcosm and macrocosm, and said that fully developed man represents the Universe in miniature. Thus to awaken myself to my own presence in the world, is to approach the understanding of the Universe *from the inside*, and no longer from the outside.

Q. – When I realise that I am asleep, if it seems to me that I am about to wake up, how can I discern the role of imagination?

A. – I can't, and that is why I need the help of others, to the extent that they are less asleep than me.

Q. – How should one look at this sort of dream in which we are engulfed, and which is so difficult to get away from?

A. – This dream is the natural state of man. We live in this dream as we live in the air, and it would be hopeless if we were not able to realise sometimes that we live not only in this world, but also in another world, where it is possible for us to awaken to different perceptions, to another way of being, of thinking and of feeling. The act of waking up can change everything: it is to be born to another world within oneself.

Q. – Does waking up imply relationship with other people? Or does it imply another world, cut from the realities which surround it?

A. – This is an excellent question because there is often a misunderstanding on this subject. To awaken is not to isolate oneself from the world, it is not to cut ourselves from the ensemble of relationships with which we are called to exist. Very much the contrary: this awakening is a broadening, an enrichment. It is the possibility of living at the same time on different levels, of facing the demands of several levels simultaneously: That is not a *minus*, it is a *plus*.

L.D. – How do you know that Gurdjieff wishes you well?

H.T. – I feel sometimes how little I interest him – and how strongly *he takes an interest* in me. By that I measure the strength of an *intentional feeling*.

Between Flights

Q. – You suggested we should meet here at Orly? Why?

H.T. – Perhaps quite simply because it figures in the usual framework of my occupations. Gurdjieff used to say: "For the man who wishes to know himself ordinary conditions are the best." But I must admit that I have a special and highly questionable affection for airports.

Q. – Why?

H.T. – An airport, this place of passage, is a revelation in itself of modern man's perpetual dispersion. In that sense we are in total "utopia" here.

Q. – What do you mean by that?

H.T. – Utopia means literally "nowhere". We are nowhere. And what is extraordinary when one travels is to find onself in one airport or another and in the end it is always the same: whether it is Tokyo, Heathrow or Kennedy Airport one is always in the same airport, connected by shuttle from one building to another.

Q. – That's not being nowhere: that's being in an airport!

H.T. – A place of departure. And more than that. Not only airports, but air travel lends itself to this kind of thought. I am nowhere and at the same time I am somewhere, and this somewhere is always me. Whether I find myself over the Atlantic, in France or in Africa; whether I find myself between two landscapes in the clouds at 5000 metres altitude, the moment I catch myself again I am always in this same body which serves as the link between my experiences. It is a way of trying in some way, somehow, to remember myself; this self-remembering which is not dependent on conditions always being the same.

Q. But these conditions – is it better for them to be always the same, or is it better for them to change?

H.T. – This is one of the questions we ask ourselves every day. So long as I am very closely associated with the very imperious conditions which punctuate my ordinary life, it seems that I have few

(an interview with Henri de Turenne for a French television programme, produced by Jean-Claude Lubtchansky, presented by Pierre Schaeffer, September 1978)

chances to wake up. Shifts are necessary. Experiences are needed
where I find myself out of my usual context. Perhaps both are needed.
Perhaps it is necessary to take off like a plane from one's habitual
ground in order to realize what one's habitual ground is.

Q. – How did you come to the teaching?

H.T. – That would take too long to explain, but, in one sense, I
could answer you quite simply: it was through Malraux.* It was
Malraux who led me to Gurdjieff.

Q. – He knew him?

H.T. – No, he did not know him.

Q. – Did he know of his existence?

H.T. – Probably . . . even certainly, but Malraux did not himself
know that he had led me to Gurdjieff. I will tell you a little about the
circumstances. I was a journalist at the time, responsible with others,
in Madrid and Barcelona, for a Republican press agency during the
Civil War and I had Malraux's book, *L'Espoir*,** as bedside reading. I
must tell you that even before I met Malraux or his books I was looking
for something, and this search was going on during my time in Spain.
Now, I came upon a reply of Garcia, who is Malraux's mouthpiece in
L'Espoir, to a question put by the Italian airman who had landed on the
Republican front line, and who asks Garcia point blank "but what can
one do better with one's life?" and the immediate, striking reply
comes: *"transform into consciousness as wide an experience as possible."*

This was for me like a thunderbolt and when I found myself in
France again with what remained of the Republican Army, I went
straight to a friend who I knew could lead me in this direction: so, I
have Malraux to thank for that.

Q. – This direction was Gurdjieff's then. Was he in Paris at the
time?

H.T. – He was in Paris and friends who were in touch with him,
Philippe Lavastine and René Daumal in particular, had already
spoken to me about him. Therefore it seemed quite natural, the
moment this note had sounded in me, to go and find them and to ask
for their help. Through them I was put in touch with Gurdjieff's
teaching and then with Gurdjieff himself.

Q. – What was Gurdjieff's attitude towards the outside world,
towards society, towards the family? Did he have a moral code?

H.T. – Certainly he had a moral code, one which sprang from a
much broader attitude towards man. He thought that if man is on

* *André Malraux, (1901-1976), French novelist, critic and politician.*
** *Days of Hope (1938)*

earth it is not by chance, that he has a mission to accomplish and that this mission implies, first and foremost, that he returns to himself, rejoins himself, awakens to himself and *is himself* as much as possible.

Q. – What was his idea of good and evil?

H.T. – The very opposite of Manicheism, his idea of good and evil was defined very precisely in relation to awakening, to that attempt to be conscious. Anything that can hinder this attempt can be considered as "evil"; anything that can help it can be considered as "good", but always "on condition that . . .", on condition that man re-discovers this fundamental impulse to be himself and as a result to know *who* he is, in order to be more himself.

Q. – But that seems to me extremely dangerous: a basis for pure egoism.

H.T. – It can appear egoistical, but in fact the worst obstacle to this search is petty egoism. A man needs to have a considerable amount of determination already to bring him to want to know himself, when everything is inviting him to run away from himself. It is a form of asceticism. What is more, if a man becomes aware of his presence in the world, he cannot in any way dissociate himself from the world: very much the contrary. He understands that this taking possession of himself demands from him that he tries to re-discover a true relationship with all the forces upon which he depends.

But if the truth be known, there is another kind of escape, which is much more serious: that of the monk or the hermit. I mean by that the escape of the man who withdraws from the world and builds a world closed in upon itself. Perhaps he wishes to open himself to God, but at the same time he takes refuge from everything – pitilessly, by breaking all the ties which make him be what he is normally called to be . . . Because it is perfectly true that in essence man is a social animal.

Q. – And Gurdjieff was entirely against that?

H.T. – Absolutely.

Q. – Does one simply become aware that these normal rules correspond to something profound in oneself, or does one discover that this is another moral code?

H.T. – Everything changes the moment an experience felt as more real bases itself on *awakening to oneself*. An awakening to oneself does not mean awakening only to the outer form of the way in which I live: it means also an awakening to what I carry in myself in the depths of my being.

Q. – You say you are a seeker, but what are you seeking?

H.T. – That is a question I ask myself every day . . . In fact, if I try to define what I am seeking, I am very quickly in danger of taking the wrong road. Perhaps there is a way of searching which compels me and I try to conform to it – but the moment I try to formulate it, I yield to a temptation which diverts me from my real search.

Q. – So it is search without hope, without aim or is there, after all, something at the end?

H.T. – That is a very good question. Is there something at the end? What is my aim? What I am seeking, above all, if you like, is *to find a direction again*. Not so much to formulate an aim to be arrived at, but rather to re-establish contact within myself with an orientation I consider to be right.

Q. – What is your motivation then? You do have a motivation?

H.T. – Without any doubt. What motivates my search is a certain dissatisfaction. Something which is not in place. I do not feel at ease in myself. I have not invented this. I have not projected it. It is something which has imposed itself on me – for example in the form of a question: Why am I here? What is the meaning of my presence here on earth? And from that moment I am already in a state of search.

Q. – But isn't everybody perhaps like that?

H.T. – Everybody is like that more or less unconsciously.

Q. – So what is the difference between *your* search and that of a scientist for example? Do you despise the results they obtain?

H.T. – Why should we despise them? I think the real problem is that these results, however normal and justified they may be, are not "integrated".

I remember reading a book a few years ago which was called *Some Seekers Question Themselves* – a collection of thoughts coming from various physicists, chemists, psychologists, metaphysicians, artists. *Some Seekers Question Themselves* . . . After all it is their function to question themselves, it seems. But it was a book which was one of a collection whose aim was to make people aware of the great human uncertainties of our time. One could say that the most shared thing in the world today *is* uncertainty. How does any one of us welcome uncertainty? Perhaps we have learnt to live with it quite well, but it stays there and cannot but continually, secretly, visit us and put us, very rightly, into a state of questioning. And in vain one is tempted to escape from the fact that at the heart of uncertainty one is led to question oneself again and again on the meaning of one's own presence on this earth.

Q. – Don't you think there are several paths to this truth which everyone is looking for?

H.T. – Without doubt. But man lacks the faculty of making good use of the knowledge he accumulates. Uncertainty remains. For the real question, isn't it, is "who am I"? Even if, when this question arises in me, I can only catch hold of it for a moment. There are other forms of creation on earth which are not there to question themselves. They are content simply with being. But man is not content simply with being. Man is here to question himself on the very meaning of his being and his destiny.

Q. – This, I think, is what all the religions do and everyone asks himself this question at least once in his life. It is not, therefore, the question itself which is specific to the teaching of Gurdjieff but the way in which you approach it?

H.T. – Yes. What is specific to it, then? What is "original" about it? Here we must be very careful not to go astray. It is one of the overwhelming tendencies nowadays, isn't it, where art and literature are concerned, this desperate search for "originality"? Oh well! Why not? Let's talk about this search for the original – and why not give it back its proper meaning of "return to origins". And what is most authentically *original* in our search is a recognition of what is absolutely essential to man. And in this we connect again with the methods of search which were those of the great traditions.

Q. – You say that all men are dissatisfied, which seems obvious to me: they all ask themselves the question "who am I?" and have done so for thousands of years and will continue to do so . . . Dissatisfaction is growing these days, it seems, at an alarming rate. One sees so many young people abandoning everything and running away to the country . . . becoming hippies and so on . . .

H.T. – Yes. What is most interesting is that it has become so acute that it cannot but lead us and particularly young people to look for solutions outside those offered by society and "the establishment."

Q. – But you think that Gurdjieff had found the answer?

H.T. – Gurdjieff was a seeker of truth. In his book, *Meetings with Remarkable Men,* he speaks about a brotherhood of Seekers of Truth to which he belonged and one might say that he was trying to make *us* seekers of truth. He sought by his own example to awaken in us the essential meaning of this search.

Q. – Was he alone, or did he belong to a brotherhood – and what do you mean by "a brotherhood"?

H.T. – This is one of the questions which has often been asked and often asked in a wrong way. He did indeed speak of a brotherhood of Seekers of Truth. To what extent did this brotherhood exist? It certainly did exist, perhaps not in the form in which he presented it, but that is not very important. One could make historical studies on the subject – many of course have been attempted, but I think each time they end up in a blind alley, because truth sought in this way does not belong to the seeker's own truth.

Q. – So, in ordinary, everyday language: does this search give an explanation of life? and in which domain?

H.T. – One could start from the place where a man finds himself lost. He "finds himself lost": it is a strange expression. He finds himself in a position where he does not know who he is, nor how to place himself in relation to the world around him. And at that moment he tries to awaken to what he really is, and it is this awakening which Gurdjieff proposes to us. His method is based entirely on an inner movement which he calls "self-remembering" . . .

Q. – Wouldn't "self awareness" be the equivalent?

H.T. – Certainly one could find a whole series of equivalents and each time it would be necessary to try to understand them anew, because, for instance, self-remembering is not a recapitulation of all the events of my past life: it is an act by which I make contact with myself again in the very moment.

Q. – But what is yourself? How can you know it, since everything is relative, since you are conditioned by everything which surrounds you?

H.T. – This is precisely what cannot really be talked about in ordinary, discursive terms. It cannot be explained. All I can say is that to know what self-remembering is I have to remember myself. At that moment I rejoin in myself a kind of knowledge which is usually completely obliterated by what is suggested to me by all the information in which I usually put my trust.

Q. – And can one be sure that one is not mistaken?

H.T. – At the very moment one is sure. Afterwards, one no longer knows by what path one reached it, nor by what path one left it. But at the very moment itself there is only room for certainty.

Q. – And you have experienced that?

H.T. – Yes, I have, again and again. I experience it each time I find again a way of being, an inner attitude, an inner disposition which allows me to put all screens aside and to find myself, if you wish, in immediate contact, in direct touch with myself.

Q. – That seems very subjective to me . . .

H.T. – That's quite true, but let us try now to know what kind of subectivity we are talking about. For example, I think I *know myself* and that's enough for me. There is a moment of hesitation, of uncertainty, and then I say "Oh yes! That's it!" I return to the known. *I refuse the unknown*, whereas if I try to abide by the spirit of the search, if I try to do justice to this demand to search to which I awaken, then I make quite a different move. I turn towards the unknown, not as the enemy to be slain or subdued, but as my chance to be really myself. *I accept to be unknown to myself.* And what I seem to know of myself will feed this impression of what transcends it.

Q. – If I have understood correctly, the major obstacle is what Gurdjieff called "identification". Isn't being identified somewhat similar to what others nowadays call "being conditioned"?

H.T. – It is not unrelated. It seems that I am totally conditioned by my ordinary way of being by everything which is foisted on me, by the whole procession of thoughts, feelings, sensations suggested to me by my surroundings, by the memory I have of all previously received information, by this perpetual bombardment to which modern man is subjected. And the phenomenon of identification is this phenomenon of subjection to this host of influences to which he submits. It is his incapacity to remain free of this conditioning.

Q. – Why do you want to free yourself from it? Can one come to be free from it?

H.T. – Yes, one can come to it, at moments. One can at the same time submit to influences and not be at their service, not be a slave to them.

Q. – Do you think, for example, that you are not influenced, as I am, by the advertisements you see in the street?

H.T. – Good heavens, yes! How could I be outwardly free from that? The real problem is not to escape from it. Not, for example, to shut myself away somewhere where no advertising will come to trouble my sleep or my peace. My real intention is to be able to walk down the street, submit to this assault and not be affected by it. To be free to choose my thoughts, my feelings, my intentions despite this perpetual bombardment.

Q. – And you think that you are free, don't you?

H.T. – I think that I want to try to be free. And I think, once again, that the search itself matters much more than the result. Man finds his real identity as a seeker – that is to say, what gives meaning to his presence is not that he has found something, but that he goes on searching even when he has found something.

Q. – But, from what I understand, it is search for it's own sake which counts, so can one then search for anything?

H.T. – Yes, that's true. And it is exactly there that the difference in levels is to be found. It is a question of knowing in what way, in what this or that search seems to us more or less debatable, more or less suspect, and in what way another sort of search seems authentic, legitimate. The answer comes from everywhere, from the depths of

time itself. And for us it is actualised by the form of search which
Gurdjieff's teaching represents. Gurdjieff's teaching is made for our
time. It speaks to the men of our time. It takes into account, too, what
remains in the man who has not been damaged by cultural
bludgeoning, who is still capable of awakening, of re-discovering
himself, since that is what it is all about: it is not about finding
something new, but once again of *re-discovering oneself*.

Q. – What sort of solution or answer does Gurdjieff's teaching
offer?

H.T. – I think it can be said that this teaching aims essentially at
being practical: it does not provide a theoretical answer but it does
provide a method.

Q. – A practical method: recipes, then?

H.T. – Certainly not recipes; a method, yes – a way of orientating
oneself which allows one to receive an answer, a provisional answer
which is intended to give a fresh impetus to the question. That is what
fundamentally differentiates this kind of search from another. There is
the seeker who is on the lookout for an answer: this answer is bound
to close the question. There is no more to be said. And then there is the
seeker who is orientated towards a renewal of what is purest and most
essential in his search, that is to say, finally, his own attitude as a
seeker, when a man awakens to himself . . .

Q. – I would like to go back to what we were saying earlier,
because I am all the same a bit uneasy . . . I don't know if you know
that Hasidic story which tells how the Devil was walking through a
town with a little imp . . . ?

H.T. – Yes, I know the story: the one about the Devil and the imp
who were following a man in the street and suddenly see him bend
down to pick up . . . a little piece of truth. Aghast, the imp turns to the
Devil and says to him: "We've had it! It's all up with us! What shall we
do from now on?" and the Devil smiles at his naïveté and says: "Don't
worry! He may have picked up the truth . . . but now *we* are going to
help him organise it!"

Q. – So that story doesn't bother you?

H.T. – What bothers me is that the Devil will obviously help me in
his cunning way to organise the truth, suggest to me an ingenious
classification of different aspects of the problem. Whereas truth and
life are one, and life to a great extent is beyond any abstract
organisation, any pre-meditated planning.

Q. – Can one get there by oneself?

H.T. – Certainly not. One can try on one's own, try and try again,
but without help it is impossible.

Q. – So what will help you?

H.T. – One could say that what can help are the traces which may have been left in man by all the attempts made by him, since his appearance on this earth. And furthermore, these traces must be brought to light by someone who has already rediscovered them, and that is the role of someone like Gurdjieff, for instance.

Q. – You seem to be alluding to a long experience coming from the depths of antiquity.

H.T. – Talking of that, I should like to get rid of this idea that Gurdjieff's teaching sets itself apart from, or in opposition to, traditional teachings. In fact it refers to what he calls the Fourth Way and the Fourth Way exists in Christianity, in Hinduism, in Islam as well as any other traditional way, Taoist or other which has as its aim to awaken man to the consciousness of his real destiny.

Q. – So is it a religion, a new religion, or the same one?

H.T. – The Fourth Way to which Gurdjieff refers contradicts none of them and cannot be mistaken for any one of them. It is an attempt to deepen what is proposed by the different doctrines. And this deepening follows first the line of a knowledge of *oneself*, the idea being that I cannot know anything if I do not know the knower himself, if I do not know the one who seeks to know. The first stage of awakening: man awakes to himself as seeker. He is a born seeker. In the same way that hunting is in the dog's blood, man searches – the true man, of course.

Q. – And so, when he looks at himself, what does he discover that he does not already know through psycho-analysis, or the philosophies and religions which have existed for thousands of years?

H.T. – Nowadays everyone is always after something "new". Obviously he discovers nothing new. He discovers something which could much more accurately be described as "renewal". He renews in himself the consciousness of being what he is, and at the same time a consciousness of all that separates him from what he really is, a consciousness much more accurate, much more impartial, more direct, of all the false mechanisms which prevent him from being truly himself.

Q. – One thing which has struck me is that Gurdjieff, as far as I know, created groups here and there when he was in Russia, in France and elsewhere, and that always at a certain moment, there seems to have been a break between him and his disciples. Did that come from him? Did he intend it or was it they who separated from him?

H.T. – It could be said that after a certain time a group was bound to break up. After a certain time, if it had begun to become a habit, if there was something which looked like an "organisation of the truth", Mr Gurdjieff was the first to break the mould. It could also be said that what he was proposing was not within everybody's reach, in the sense that the moment one understood what it was all about it was enough to fill you with fear and take flight. So there were flights, evasions and refusals to go on.

Q. – That is the disciples' side of it, but I don't understand Gurdjieff's side, because, according to what you are saying he was just as capable of breaking habits, breaking routine, breaking the shell. So if this was rejected did he consider the case to be hopeless?

H.T. – Not at all. The moment there was a danger of stultification he would shuffle the cards, so to speak, and begin again at zero. It was not hopeless at all, on the contrary, it was the reappearance of life just when we were threatened with falling into a rut or becoming paralysed.

Q. – Do you have the feeling that this teaching is a bit like a way reserved for the élite?

H.T. – In a sense, yes, but it would still be necessary to know how to define this élite, because it is very clear that most men do not want to be bothered by untimely questions, and when they do come across them, they run away from them as fast as they can. "Who am I?" in its true sense is not a question for everyone.

Q. – I find this rather shocking, because the Catholic religion, for example, at least gives everyone a chance to save his soul.

H.T. – There is a chance for everyone, but "everyone" does not want it.

Q. – "Many are called but few are chosen"?

H.T. – I understand very well what is behind your question. There is something repulsive in the idea that those who are chosen believe that they are chosen, and consider themselves chosen and keep themselves to themselves. But what was so characteristic of Mr Gurdjieff was the way in which he ultimately welcomed *anyone*.

Q. – Yes, but all the same there is a side which is a little hidden, esoteric. The door is not exactly wide open. Why?

H.T. – Simply in order to respect a certain conformity to laws. There are some things which can only take place in a minimum of quietness. It is essential that the conditions lend themselves to the attempt to awaken and be present to oneself, and the mutual aid, the exchanges which are inherent to this search cannot take place anywhere and anyhow.

Q. – Intellectual comfort from the outset, all the same.

H.T. – That is the risk, of course, but I wouldn't say "intellectual comfort" . . . In fact, it was striking: most of the time, when with Gurdjieff, the intellectuals seemed rather handicapped, crippled. Whereas someone who had been lucky enough to be brought up in an environment less artificial, closer to that of a peasant or a sailor, say, found he had a common ground for communication with him, while the intellectual was always uselessly going about it in the wrong way in order to get to the same place. But what swept away these differences of formation, of education, these "subjective particularities" was the real, immediate effect that Gurdjieff had on us. He was there, in front of us, and beneath his gaze each one of us tried to wake up. What did he expect from us? Perhaps that what he himself was seeking should resound in us like an echo. He was there, in front of us, as a living example of the seeker which every man is destined to re-discover in himself. He was there, in front of us, and by his presence, his insistence, sometimes silent, sometimes accompanied by words, he tried to call forth what he himself was experiencing as an urgent, inner necessity.

Q. – But if the master is no longer there, what does one do?

H.T. – This links with the question you asked earlier. He has played his role. He has withdrawn from the scene. Does this mean that his influence has suddenly come to an end? Does it mean that the masters, in the different traditions, who while alive were like beacons to their disciples, cease, once they are dead, to accompany with their light those who, down the centuries, try in their turn to follow the path which they opened to them?

If, in fact, as Montaigne said: "Every man carries within him the entire form of the human condition", then I carry Gurdjieff in me. No doubt most of the time I am unable to find him again, but, perhaps, in seeking a corresponding attitude, in trying to feel myself as more available in that attitude, I can re-discover in myself the Gurdjieff I knew and who has never ceased to exert his influence on me.

A Question of Balance

(An interview for PARABOLA magazine)

Former journalist and photographer, who also worked at the Musée de l'Homme in Paris, Henri Tracol has been for many years one of the chief exponents of the teaching of G.I. Gurdjieff. The system taught by Gurdjieff includes within it a complex elaboration of the place of food on cosmological and psychological levels. We sought out Mr. Tracol in his summer retreat in the south of France to speak with him about these ideas in the light of his own long experience. He greeted us in his shaded courtyard where among the trees, herbs, and flowers were several of his large stone sculptures – massive forms smoothed out of a local white stone. His latest work, "Ganesha," awaited final polishing in an open-air studio adjoining the main house.

Once inside the cool, high-ceilinged living room, we sat together at a large, old wooden table. Mr Tracol responded to our questions with great interest and intensity. Gentle, unpretentious, direct, full of quick humour, he seemed somehow to accompany his words. As we spoke, the exchange became not only a discussion of abstract ideas but a kind of nourishment in itself.

Lorraine Kisly

Parabola – We might start out by speaking about physical food. In the United States now, perhaps in Europe as well, there is a great interest in experimentation – in macrobiotics, in vegetarianism, in organically grown foods, and it becomes almost a moral issue what sort of food we eat. But in the Gospels Christ says: "For what goes into your mouth, that will not defile you, but that which issues from your mouth – it is that which will defile you." Does it make a difference what sort of food we eat?

Henri Tracol – It certainly does. Now, what is the point of view from which we could evaluate this first food, physical food? Of course, we cannot be without a certain discrimination about what is good or bad from an ordinary point of view. But what is more important? First, this question can be understood only in relationship to the whole. You have to be attentive to your food, and not only the first food, but to the others. Whether you know it or not, you depend very much on what you eat, and breathe, and so on. It is not only necessary for the physical body, but also for the whole of your being. Food is needed not just to sustain your physical existence, it's also for other purposes. It is not to be belittled. Now, of course, you can eat the best food, drink the best drinks, and if you do not understand what it is for, it is lost – very largely, lost. What is absorbed and what feeds you really is a very

This interview is reprinted by kind permission of the Editors of PARABOLA magazine where it first appeared in Vol. IX, No. 4, 1984 on Food.

small proportion of what is given. A small part sustains the outer existence, but most of it is wasted. Now I think of something that has been very striking for me. Perhaps you know a book by Viktor Frankl, *Man's Search for Meaning*. He speaks about the way people who were doomed to death in concentration camps could survive. What they ate was very, very little, very insignificant. But for them there was something much more important. There was a wish to be. Even though they did not fully realize the importance of it, they perceived that something was necessary, and was far more important than their comfort, their despair and so on. They knew that something was offered them, and they wanted to live. And on that basis, they could survive in conditions that were impossible – medically, impossible.

So this is what is really important, to understand that the question of food is not just an outer, mechanical process, it is also something of significance. Insofar as you are able to be attentive to this perspective, it is really of value that you do not treat this food as something insignificant.

I would also say, in another field, that there was something that Mr Gurdjieff never accepted – a completely stupid disregard for the body, or any kind of scorning of the body. He evoked a respect for the body. In the same perspective, what is really important there is not only that which we ordinarily call the body, with its pleasure, or fear of pain and so on, but the body itself as a place where something can be born again, and develop. So, it has to be respected, and its needs, its real needs, met. There are many misinterpretations of what he said or wrote about the necessity to compel the body to obey higher imperatives. It is not *against* the body, it is *for* the body. And the body knows it, too!

P. – Mr Gurdjieff has written that it is necessary to strive to have everything necessary and satisfying for the physical body. This puzzles me – not only everything necessary, but also everything satisfying. When is this possible – to have both?

H.T. – It implies the need for a degree of understanding. If we draw a list of what is necessary and what is satisfying it will be futile, of course.

It is a question of balance, mostly. And it means a balance with other needs as well. Otherwise, something can be quite satisfactory for the body itself, as separate from the rest; but it creates a lack of balance. What is necessary and what is really satisfactory is a balance between all the different needs of the being – physical, and psychological, and spiritual.

P. – So the body needs this balance in order to be truly satisfied.

H.T. – Yes.

P. – How do you see the point of the dietary restrictions that occur in so many traditions – Islam, Judaism, Buddhism? So many traditions set out very clear rules about what to eat, and when, and how much. What is the point of such rules?

H.T. Mr Gurdjieff has spoken of such rules, and of how they are always linked with other rules. It is a whole, and if something is missing in the other rules, then it is pointless. You forget what the reason is. At certain times it may be necessary to refrain from certain foods, and at other times not. In any case it is not the real point. We have to adapt ourselves to conditions – to outer conditions, of course – but to inner conditions as well. Otherwise we make fools of ourselves trying to stick to something as though it had to be followed at any cost.

P. – Did Mr Gurdjieff subscribe to any particular rules about eating?

H.T. – In *Meetings with Remarkable Men* he speaks of his encounter with an old Persian dervish at a time when he as a young man was very keen to follow certain rules; for example, in regard to the thorough chewing of food. Asked by the dervish why he was so scrupulously practising such a demanding method of eating, the young Gurdjieff explained at length why this was highly recommended by certain schools of Indian yogis. To which the old man shook his head and said, "Let God kill him who does not know and yet presumes to show others the way to the doors of His Kingdom." After explaining to his young visitor that it was imperative, at his age, not to deprive his stomach of the opportunity to exercise itself in its natural work, the old man concluded by hinting that those who recommended such mastication had, as is said, "heard a bell without knowing where the sound came from."

As a matter of fact, Mr Gurdjieff trained us to eat all sorts of things that were not particularly recommended! He would insist that you at times had to eat all sorts of greasy, fatty foods, all sorts of ingredients that would be very, very hot – which from an ordinary medical point of view were impossible to accept. Of course there were those who needed to be on a special diet and he was resilient enough to exempt them. But otherwise, you *had* to eat what was served. He would go to the market and choose the ingredients and would be preparing the food from early in the morning for the evening. He would allow very few to help him. He had his own ways. And when people were eating with him, he was very attentive to the way you took in food. It was very important for him. When he saw someone who was absorbed in a question he perhaps wanted to ask and was eating without knowing he was eating, he would frown, and sometimes scold and so on. So there was a respect for food that was necessary. No matter *what* it was!

P. – This respect for food that you mention seems to have almost completely disappeared from our lives – perhaps because most of us are so far away from the growing and raising of food, we no longer know what it has to cost for it to be available to us.

H.T. – It is true, it is not easy to obtain. But, you see, when we speak of food, we speak of one category, forgetting or neglecting the others, and I think it's misleading. In fact, there are all sorts of food, and it is a question of the whole being. There is the idea that there are three kinds of food: ordinary food, air, and impressions. You can go on existing for days without ordinary food. You can survive if you do not breathe for a few minutes perhaps, not very long. But you cannot exist one second without impressions. This idea is fantastic. One can hear it, perhaps be surprised, and say, "That's very interesting." But it's forgotten immediately, because it is not properly received. Perhaps it demands a lifetime to understand what it means. The food of impressions is taken in constantly. You need this third kind of food in order to really take in the first food. In order to breathe, you need it too. What is essential there is mostly neglected, ignored – it is fantasy for us. Of course it is closely related to another idea which very largely escapes us, and which is that only higher centers can really receive, properly, the food of impressions. Higher centers – and it is said that higher centers are fully developed in a human being. They function perfectly well. What is missing is the proper link with lower centers. In *Beelzebub*, Mr Gurdjieff speaks of what happens to this finer food of impressions. Most of it is lost. But part of it is always maintained and perceived and absorbed for the development of higher components of a being. So, without our knowing – and especially when we are asleep – something is taking place there.

P. – These impressions are being received all the time, so it is a question of digestion?

H.T. – Yes; in fact something is digested without knowing it. Regardless of what becomes of our lower centres – the higher centres need to go on existing. It is said also that accidentally – but it is not mere accident, it is for a higher purpose – we receive the necessary help for the digestion of these finer impressions. Of course I do not claim to understand this, but it does evoke something in me. So we are made use of for the sake of the higher centers, and even though we seem to be cut from them, they are there.

P. – It really does seem as though it is impossible to speak of one food at a time, as though we eat at one moment, and breathe at another and then receive an impression.

H.T. – We are enslaved by the notion of time, of course.

These questions also evoke the mystery of what is called conscious attention. Ordinarily speaking, what we call conscious attention is when we translate our experience immediately into our ordinary terms. "This is that": we define. But in fact this sort of attention is just on the border – it is superficial. It is an automatism that goes on and on, and the machine is very good. It works very well, outerly. But for the whole of the being, including the higher parts, it is almost insignificant – it deals with the outer part of our existence, that's all. For what is essential is not there. That's why it's so important to take into account what happens in very special conditions, as in the case of the prisoners Frankl speaks of. Ordinary conditions of existence are important of course, they have to be taken into account. But the real meaning is not there.

P. – It has been said that every creature is designed for a certain kind of food, and can be defined in relationship to what it eats. Each creature can be seen as a kind of specialist in eating certain foods. It seems that there might be here a kind of definition of the difference between human beings and all other beings in this question of impressions.

Are there certain kinds of impressions that only human beings can receive? Are we sort of specialists in the possibility of receiving a certain kind of food?

H.T. – Undoubtedly. Now is it for our ordinary mind to try to understand what that means? It is very dangerous, because most of the time we will translate it into terms that do not correspond. Ordinary thinking cannot cover this at all. Now, is there something that we could call higher mind? Do we know it, or do we just project an image? Is it once again a wrong work of our lower mind? It tries to define what it should be, and so on. No; I think we need to keep a kind of respect for what is given us at certain moments to perceive – not as a result of any mental combination, but something that is offered, and offered, and offered, and *for once* we perceive it. Does this perception depend on me or is this something which is granted me? I think even when it depends partly on me, it's mostly granted; and it has to be perceived as granted.

P. – Several times now you have said that our energy from all sorts of food is mostly wasted. Is anything actually wasted?

H.T. – One cannot help thinking of so much waste in nature. All the seeds which seem completely lost – but they are not lost; they serve for something, so nothing is lost, or wasted completely. But we cannot remain indifferent when we see what is *partly* wasted. What can be planted and can grow into a splendid tree – we are sensitive to the difference. It calls something in us. Something is there which could be fully developed – this evokes our real interest. And it applies to man as well. Of course he could be a very splendid animal for the Olympic Games, or a fantastic artist. But something is missed for the full stature of a being – I will not say one who could do everything, it is not the case; I mean one has been born with a certain balance of capacities which go far beyond what our ordinary imagination could conceive. But there is first of all a sense of balance, of right balance, and there is a certain balance in a moment when a man awakes to his own destiny. He is able to join with what is in him, what is there as a seed in him, and find the corresponding attitude and functioning which bear witness to the presence of this hidden capacity. It may not be corresponding to what could perhaps be expected from someone else, but it corresponds to what *he* is. I think this is a real source of commitment. I mean, not to dream of fantastic realization, but to be sensitive to the presence of the call of capacities which are there waiting for recognition, and waiting for completion.

P. – Whatever awareness is (again a word probably misunderstood), it seems that one can sense that the quality of physical food and air and impressions would all change if there was a light of awareness on the process instead of it taking place in the dark, separated somehow. This was what Mr Gurdjieff seemed to be calling for all the time.

H.T. – Oh, yes, He knew that what was usually meant there was most of the time a far distant approach – something that did not correspond really to what he was evoking. If you are not one, whole, there is always something missing. Now a person who dreams of understanding the whole makes a fool of himself – it is simply impossible. He's just dreaming. What you can try is to open to what corresponds to you, and to you only. In a way – this is, I would say, a joke – you can understand something that God cannot understand. God cannot reduce himself to become so little! The sense of specificity, of what is possible for a particular person, evokes a completely different interest from a pretense to understand more and more and more, up to the whole. It is simply stupid. It is not what is demanded. What is offered, and demanded, is to approach what corresponds to you – and to no one else. It means also that you have to share with others – there are many things to share with others. But there is something specific to you and to no one else on the earth. In centuries and centuries you are the only one who can understand in that way, that very particular and specific way. And this is really appealing. It helps us to understand that something is demanded of me.

P. – Mr Gurdjieff speaks of self-remembering very much. In reference to an earlier question, is the impression of oneself unique to human beings? Does it constitute a kind of food only humans can receive?

H.T. – Another mystery. Self-remembering . . . to awake. If we begin to think in our ordinary terms, what does it mean to awake? Do I decide at a certain time to awake? And who decides? There is no answer there, except to realize that I am awakened by something. It is not that I decide to awaken and I awake: that is simply impossible. But maybe "I," with another meaning, the real "I," reminds me, calls me back. The sense of my being: it is not something that I invent, or that I think of. It is there. And it calls me back. That's self-remembering. And on this basis, there is a certain kind of awareness which comes to me. Most of the time it's enjoyed by a part which pretends to be the owner – "Oh yes, I think that." That's a betrayal. I have been given to see something, to understand something, and I try to join with it. But if I let in this pretense to be the *one who* . . . it's spoiled. Does it mean that I have to keep passive about it? Not at all. In order to keep awake, something is demanded of me. It is demanded of the whole of me, all my faculties and capacities, including my ordinary attention, my possibilities to establish connections, associations, useful associations. On behalf of what has been given me, is being given me now, I do not allow myself to be passive. There is something behind. Something – there is no question of reaching for anything. It is not to be reached; it is there. It gives an objective meaning to my attempt at joining with what is offered me. If I keep that, if my ordinary, my outer self keeps that, is faithful to this recognition, then it's given me over and over again to discover what is proposed and proposed and proposed. Of course, it cannot last very long: but for a time it can last. I can experience it. And it leaves a trace, an alive memory is left in me which I can recapture later. This memory is given. To remember myself is memory, yes? But what will remember? It is given to me to remember and I awake again to a sense of this hidden presence.

So, food. Food of impressions – impressions of myself.

You know, when a journalist comes to interview, say, a potter, and asks him: "Well, could you explain to me how you do that?" If the potter begins to say, "Well, first this and then that . . . and so on" what does it convey? But if the potter goes on with his pot, the answer is there without an explanation – without reducing it to explanation. It can be perceived. And then the journalist who is really a journalist would also try with his tools to translate what had been perceived into something which could be read. He *saw* the process. But most of the time it is stupidities. I do not know what objective art is, but at least I know that those who pretend to explain are neither artists – nor objective witnesses! Very often we *seem* to understand and very often it's misappropriation – "Oh yes, I understand." It is given me to understand at a moment when I am sensitive to what is offered me. But as soon as I take hold of it, it's finished.

But it's marvelous, isn't it? You know, the person who understands everything always, has an explanation for everything – he's dead!

P. – On a larger scale, I'm wondering if you feel there is a relationship between the idea of reciprocal feeding on a cosmic scale and the idea of the three foods.

H.T. – Part of it is certainly the question of scale. It cannot be approached without keeping the sense of relativity. In the representation of a human being, for example, it is said that the human mind is thirty thousand times slower than the body. You understand what it means. "Oh, yes, of course." But you don't. It's out of scale for our ordinary way of thinking. We can talk about it – but we do not understand. And there are times we can perceive something corresponding – but there is something which is always late, it comes afterwards. It's a reflection of a reflection – dimmer and dimmer, so slow, and so many things have passed in between. So once again we are in front of this mystery that is far beyond what we are able to conceive of. Yet these questions have a value, provided of course we do not attempt to answer them. But it may be a help to enlarge the scale of our interrogation. What we are given to perceive in our normal surroundings is a reflection of a reflection of a reflection of something much greater and much bigger. It is really of value to understand that what is taking place here is insignificant in a way, and at the same time it is extremely significant for me if I see it the other way round. I am a small piece of life which is invisible on this larger scale. So if I begin to *think* about it, and to draw conclusions – I think I need to keep a sense of wonder. When I quote an objective thought from a great thinker, if I just quote it, I spoil it. But if I capture the sense of wonder, I know that I do not understand, but I know that it opens my understanding; it opens it to more – always more. Then I feel myself closer to what was offered.

There are certain formulations I can think of that even if I live twenty more years, I am sure I will not be able to understand. There are things which are unfathomable, but each time it evokes so much in me that it's a rediscovery each time. I don't understand why sometimes we try so hard to get it understood. It would kill something in me. The sense of wonder once again is very much more.

P. – There seems to be an appetite of the mind, a kind of greed it has when it is working alone and isolated which wants its own satisfaction without any regard to the rest of the being.

H.T. – There is certainly a greed for impressions, but this greed is against a real reception. It is true that the mind has this avidity. Now there is always the possibility of referring to something which is behind. I think that attitudes, outerly expressed by tension – (*leans forward, slamming table*) – "What do you mean?" For me that means it is finished; it makes it impossible for other impressions to come and to awake corresponding spheres of interest in my mind, in my body, and in my feeling. But these awaken insofar as I am able to remember the amplitude of the gift which is offered me again and again. If I succumb to my ordinary pretense and greed and I lose something; but if I try to keep open to what I know is there, whether I am aware of it or not – it is there. Then there is a natural attempt at keeping open – I keep open. I know that something is offered me over and over again and I try not to be away from it.

P. – So there is a kind of fasting which is possible for the mind, a not allowing the greed of the mind, the greed of the feeling, the greed of the body to overtake this openness.

H.T. – Yes, fasting. Keeping available for what cannot satisfy my ordinary greed. Memory is there also to help me – a certain kind of memory. Memories are against it most of the time. But there is memory in depth that we can try to open ourselves to once again, and once again. We lack corresponding words – in the same breath we speak of memory and memory, real memory and false memory. But it is there.

L.D. – What is, in your opinion, your role now? (The exterior role you play in life?)

H.T. – Outwardly, to struggle for the conquest of what is called a stable situation in life on a scale which goes with the person I owe it to myself to represent for my near and dear ones.

As for the story of my relationship with this role – it is not without some misunderstandings . . . At the outset, the necessity to embark at all costs brought me at the same time great worries (because of my repeated failures) and the excitement of risk, of adventure, of as yet unattempted experience. That is to say, I often let myself get caught in the game. Later, in spite of the dangers increased by the very volume of my undertakings, my more and more frequent successes gave me confidence: there again, I often let myself be caught in the trap. Today – when I stroll through unknown provincial streets to deal with things which no longer have the attraction of novelty, nor the spice of danger, I have more than ever the impression of lugging a lifeless dummy about. But the most terrible thing, Luc, is that inwardly there is nothing. Nothing at all. How do I feel behind the mask? Empty. And despair is on the look-out for me. I must at all cost find reasons for myself in order to carry on. And not only of the "any old kind" sort. I find myself laughing bitterly at this "struggle for a stable situation." I also find myself retrieving the sense of it and rediscovering hope. For I have already received unhoped-for experiences and lessons "from life itself." But what I await, above all, over all, from my material success, is a vigorous impetus in my inner work – in order to make a balance.

George Ivanovitch Gurdjieff:
Man's Awakening and the Practice of
Remembering Oneself

George Ivanovitch Gurdjieff. Yes indeed, I knew this man. I was among those who, during the German occupation of France, frequented his modest apartment off the avenue des Ternes in Paris. Others have described the sumptuous "feasts of friends" to which we were bidden several times a week and which, to say the least, were incongruous in those hard times.

To see him in the early morning busying himself in getting the rarest and most exotic provisons the market could produce and preparing with such care, on his old charcoal stove, the most harmoniously audacious meals, was to realise what importance he attached to the patriarchal custom of welcoming guests. It was his own way to make us sense, beyond the turmoil of contradictory reactions that such hospitality inevitably aroused in us at such a period, the exceptional character of those hours – so remote from our ordinary lives – that we spent with him. And the subtle flavour of his dishes and the vodka in which the famous "toasts to the idiots" were drunk, merged, on another scale, with the special nourishment which we could receive only from him.

"Potlatch"* some people called it, and not without reason. There is no doubt at all that in this generous display of hospitality there was an element of provocation. And later we shall have occasion to return to this question. But what was the challenge implicit in this largesse? What summons in disguise? What was there to understand? There we were, time after time, back at his side, returning as prodigal children to a father until then unknown – suddenly astonished to be there, taking things for granted, astonished but – it must be admitted – a little uneasy at our inability to grasp the reason why. For if he accepted us as his children what was he likely to expect from us in return?

(Lecture given at the Salle du Musée de l'Homme, Paris, in March 1967 at the request of the Society "L'Homme et la Connaissance", revised edition 1987.)

* "Potlatch": a tribal feast given by a chieftain for the express purpose of challenging his guests. This custom, originally found among the Kwakiutl Indians of British Columbia, is considered by many anthropologists to be one of the main features of what they are pleased to call "primitive mentality". "Author's note"

Nothing, it seemed, except, as a first step, to open our eyes and recognise him as indeed our father.

At this point, I am tempted to recall his massive presence, the serene power, at once formidable and reassuring, which emanated from his whole being – his bearing, his gestures, his manner. I can still hear his voice resounding in me, arousing echoes that are ever fresh and new. Above all, I find myself standing before him, his eyes in mine, confronting the exacting benevolence of his gaze. Exacting, yes, and kindling with fire and often merciless. He seemed to guess the best as well as the worst in us and, being an expert in such matters, he smiled. That smile was ironic and compassionate but quite without indulgence. Nothing escaped him. We felt that he would not hesitate to show himself as pitiless to the self-torturers which, unknowingly, we were. This is really what can be called: to love.

He listened and invited us to open ourselves. But sentimentality and maudlin beneficence had no part in him – no doubt about that. To be indulgent was not in his nature. His language was rough, his tone sometimes violent, his comments could be brutal, his mimicry and gestures all too eloquent. And his sudden resumption of affability could be even more wounding. In short, he did not spare us.

There is no lack of material to illustrate this uncompromising side of his nature. But all this belongs to the past . . .

I knew this man, I said just now. But was I not, more or less wittingly, lying? Who can say of any man that he has really known him?

Properly speaking, one's knowledge of man begins with oneself. Only in so far as I know myself can I find again the mark of Gurdjieff's imprint upon me – the trace of the impressions that he left in me according to what I happened to be during the nine years I spent near him. And I realise what these impressions have become according to what I myself have become.

The image of the same man is inevitably different for everyone who comes into contact with him, and since the image is necessarily created by the beholder, it is subject to change and fluctuates according to the beholder's idiosyncrasies. It would be fruitless, therefore, from various personal reminiscences, subjective and fragmentary as they are, to attempt to reconstruct what could only be the robot-portrait of a ghost.

If we are seeking Gurdjieff it is not in this direction that we shall find him. There are other indications that can orientate us better. Is it not a fact, for instance, that for a number of our contemporaries the encounter with this man was the major event in their lives? Even when some of them later drifted away, were they not secretly still intrigued, even wondering if all they had experienced had truly happened and whether they had really lived through it all? And was it not common to us all, this sense of having missed almost everything that he could offer us? After all, what we came to look for in Gurdjieff was not the man – it was the Master.

Or, to put it more clearly (for nothing could be worse at this juncture than to create artificial distinctions) it was the man *in his quality of Master*. At the risk of overstating my case let me tell you of an experience which accurately bears on this ambiguity, an experience that was shared by someone who is present tonight.

Mr Gurdjieff had invited the two of us to lunch in the rue des Colonels Renard, and we found ourselves alone with him – a rare enough event and one not to be missed. I arrived, full of burning questions, and found him so benevolent, so manifestly disposed to listen that I watched eagerly for the first opportunity to put them to him. But the opportunity never came.

Obviously he had detected my impatience and so proceeded to play with me as a cat plays with a mouse. He was disarmingly gentle and benign but the moment he sensed that I was ready to return to the charge, he ingeniously side-tracked me, either with some malicious comment or a witty anecdote, or by challenging me to detect a specific flavour or to guess the exact quantity of spices used in a certain dish he had devised for our special benefit.

I was at a loss to understand where all these manoeuvres were leading. My questions suddenly lost all their weight. Never shall I forget his look of amusement as he watched the skirmishes of the battle surging in me, nor my feelings of frustration and distress that were nevertheless permeated by a strange gratitude for this lesson. When at length I found myself once more out in the street, I felt like Parsifal in the desert waste after the Fisher King's castle had vanished.

Who among us did not suffer from this "Parsifal complex" – as I was pleased to call it from then on – during those wonderfully rich years when so much was given and so little really received?

There is certainly nothing new in this. Even so, it is a serious matter – all the more serious when the voice we did not know how to listen to is now forever silenced.

After the death of a Master, what becomes of his disciples and the teaching he has transmitted to them? It depends. What kind of a Master do we speak of here and what kind of disciple? If his disciples inaugurate a cult, become sectarian or fanatical, freeze his thought and codify his slightest utterance – can such a situation relate to a real Master?

But when he who has gone has taken such care, during his

lifetime, to warn his followers of the danger of any kind of crystallisation and the everlasting necessity of putting everything in question, even at the risk of leaving them in a continuing dilemma – this is a very different matter.

According to a former "Gurdjieffian", it was Gurdjieff's failure that he never trained a single disciple who was capable of understanding what was expected of him.

Margaret Anderson, who quotes this sombre reflection, hastens to put this in doubt when she asserts that she knew "at least three people fully trained to transmit the essence of Gurdjieff's teaching, one of whom had worked with him for more than thirty years and had been entrusted by him to pursue his task after his death".

But we must go further. If it is true that the tree is known by its fruit (and who will deny that this is so?), it is too often forgotten that only a true gardener understands trees and fruits. Who will pretend to be an expert here? And where can such a one be found? There will be no lack of candidates for this role, promising or unpromising, as the case may be. But their knowledge for the most part, will be hearsay.

A true gardener's first care is to make sure that the tree is still alive and capable of bearing fruit. He will not be disconcerted when one bough fails and another matures, for he knows that he is not here dealing with a diagram or a botanical chart but with life itself. God's gardener knows well that he himself has created nothing, he has merely dug the ground, planted the tree, hoed, watered and pruned – all this after taking into account the nature of the soil, the atmospheric conditions, the climate and the prevailing wind. And if he has trained some assistants, they will know, when one day he has to leave them, how to watch over the tree that is now in their keeping.

Is it, moreover, so difficult for us to realise that there must inevitably be long years of struggle between "seeing what is expected of us" and being able in some measure to put it into practice? Which – by the way – accounts for many defections.

Furthermore, is it, in the last analysis, so difficult to accept the obvious – that Gurdjieff would have failed in his most essential task had he, in fact, "trained a disciple" capable of understanding *once and for all* what life itself, and his own deepest being, would unceasingly exact from him to the very end?

These questions show us without any doubt how far we are today from understanding the concept of Master.

One could speak, in vague terms, of his "message" or of his "mission". But to underline the fact that he is there for a purpose, that he has something to do, an exacting task to accomplish, opens the way to a quite different approach. One step further, and the Master will appear to us not only as having a precise role to play in a particular context but, in the long run, as the embodiment of the role itself.

Indeed, the Master is one with his function. It can even be said that he *is* the function, the function made man.

But what is the essence of this many-faceted function that forever eludes our grasp?

You know, or at least can surmise, the answer. It is suggested in the title given to the subject we are studying this evening. The master-function is that of Bodhidharma whose role was to waken the sleeper. The Master is the Awakener.

Yes. The Master embodies awakening.

But who is to be awakened? From what, and to what?

The Master awakens those who themselves wish to wake up. He rouses them from their sleep, awakes them to Being, to Reality, to Life.

Everything has to start with an encounter. But who is it that desires this encounter? An event of this kind cannot be entirely due to chance. The least it requires is that both sides are ready for it. Otherwise, even if the encounter takes place, the necessary contact cannot be made.

We cannot speak of a Master without disciples any more than of disciples without a Master. What makes a Master is not only his power to transmit the truth he himself has received; it is also the expectation of a few.

René Daumal, Luc Dietrich and their fellow searchers were properly qualified to be true disciples, for they were hungry and athirst. Their search for the truth was based on an essential dissatisfaction, a profound unease and a particular suffering brought about by not really being what they were, nor what they felt themselves called to be. The sleepers were tossing in their beds, fumbling for the light.

Unless there is someone at hand to shake them, only those sleepers who really wish to wake will be woken. As for the others – well, there is no sounder sleeper than the man who does not want to wake up.

And from where does this wish to awake arise? Something must be glimmering under the cinders, some embers still be glowing. Awakening is already smouldering under the ashes of the dreams of the one who seeks to awake.

This is the prime mystery, the fundamental enigma, as if awakening were already there, watching for the propitious moment to shake its sleeper.

But there are few who know how to recognise the nature of this waking dream which is our substitute for life.

The old Taoist Master, Chuang Tzu, well understood this when he asked:

> "Is life not a dream?
> There are some who, when awakened from a happy dream, are desolate. Others, delivered from a sad dream, rejoice. In either case, so long as the dream lasted they believed in its reality.
> So it is with the great awakening, death, after which we say of life that it was nothing but a long dream. But, among the living, there are few who understand this. Almost everyone believes himself to be awake. Some are convinced that they are kings, others that they are paupers. You and I, all of us dream. I who tell you that you dream, I too dream my dream."

For the moment let us be content with this brief reference to Chuang Tzu, lest some Taoist in exile should come along claiming to be the begetter of Gurdjieff's teaching, as indeed happened recently when, almost simultaneously, a theologian of the Eastern Christian Church and a "Sufi" under mandate from a secret brotherhood in the Middle East made the same assertion.

Be that as it may, the sleep which Gurdjieff speaks of as the permanent condition of the man who believes himself to be awake, is a kind of hypnotic trance in which he is imprisoned by the power of imagination, in order to prevent his awakening and seeing himself for what he is.

As to the final aim of Awakening, what it leads to, could I say more than any serious searcher does not know already? Under many diverse aspects there is but one aim, just as a mountain has only one summit.

In referring to Being, Reality, Life, I was not yielding to the power of words. Their inner resonance is not the same for all of us and each can get intoxicated in his own way. This is not our object.

It is, rather, to confront a concept on which we may, I hope, find ourselves at one – the idea of *return*. Awakening is not the conquest of a state of higher consciousness. It is a movement, repeatedly attempted and repeatedly denied, a return to the consciousness of *what is*.

Even the most fleeting glimmer of consciousness carries the promise of a participation in All that Exists, "out of which, by division and differentiation," as Gurdjieff says, "springs the diversity of all observable phenomena."

But let us not dally with words that lend themselves all too easily to pseudo-metaphysical speculations. Seen in its true spiritual perspective, Gurdjieff's teaching is essentially *practical*.

And since we seek to comprehend the function of Awakening as it appears in a Master we should now try to understand how it proceeds.

Is it not his first concern to assemble or create the best possible conditions for awakening? Nor should we forget that he himself is part of these conditions, he is integral to them, or rather, he deliberately puts himself under their sway. He is, in fact, the central condition towards which others gravitate.

We may then be less astonished by the freedom with which Gurdjieff juggled with these conditions. For to him, it seems, all means were good. The simplest and most evident was his own presence – the silent influence he exercised on all who came to him, which sometimes assumed a very direct form, as a sort of osmosis.

But he had many other means up his sleeve, indirect and, to outward appearances, negative.

For example, he never hesitated to arouse doubts about himself by the kind of language he used, by his calculated contradictions and by his behaviour – to such a point that people around him, particularly those who had a tendency to worship him blindly, were finally obliged to open their eyes to the chaos of their own reactions.

Awakening implies a rupture in the thread of continuity, a change of levels, an interval between two completely different states. A shock is necessary to ensure the passage from one state to the other.

This shock could be brought about in all sorts of ways – by an abrupt change of attitude, by direct provocation or an unexpected smile, by a redoubling of exacting requirements or a sudden mollifying gesture.

Naturally, all these methods presuppose the existence of a science, of a gifted hand and a consummate artistry on the part of the manipulator. Beware of Sorcerers' Apprentices, who imagine they can follow on and imitate their masters! Sooner or later they have to give up or else learn to adapt. Such capacities cannot be transmitted, even to those who may be qualified to receive them. They have to be found for oneself, adjusted to one's own capacities and made to accommodate to our constantly changing circumstances.

In any case, Gurdjieff's teaching was as far away as it is possible to get from all didactic formalism. With him, in him, doctrine and method formed a close, indissoluble union. His refusal to meet our expectations of a "teaching" couched in orderly terms and following a "rational" sequence, was in itself a lesson. He had the art of eluding questions, only to offer a masterly answer, when we had already given up all hope of receiving any.

He spoke of his "system", and yet opposed all systematization.

Here we come to a point that has to be very clearly understood. It is no part of the Master's role to take over the disciple's effort of understanding; the latter, and he alone, must make it for himself. The shocks, suggestions and situations calculated to provoke the disciple's awakening are there solely to prepare and train him to do without his master, to go forth under his own steam as soon as he shows himself capable of doing so.

By its very nature, the inner search is inevitably an individual matter. The suggestion is put, the call is made. The rest is up to each one of us.

On the one hand – sleep, absence, forgetfulness; on the other, awakening, presence and remembering oneself. These are the basic elements of the problem. It is up to each of us to join in the game.

But what does it mean to remember oneself?

Without launching into a lengthy dissertation let me, nevertheless, at this point, try to dispel some possible misconceptions.

If we have chosen this theme above all others to elaborate upon, it is because the practice of remembering oneself is the master key to Gurdjieff's teaching. It is the Alpha and Omega, the threshold that must be passed at the outset and crossed and recrossed time and again. It is also the musical "silent pause"* of complete realisation, since any man capable of reaching it would know in their entirety the inner and outer relationships of which it consists. He would be completely himself and able at last to take his true place in the Universe.

It must also be said that remembering oneself admits of an infinite number of approaches. It can be looked at from many and varied angles, it has certain definite degrees and stages and there is always more in it than we can ever grasp.

Yet, beneath all its multiple forms we can savour again and again the unique taste of this fundamental experience. Nothing else matters and it is because this fact is not sufficiently realised that so many discordant notes are heard.

There is a time for everything – for meditation with doors and eyelids closed, as well as for plunging with eyes wide open into the vortex of life. Crystallisation, arbitrary division, dissociation, wrong

---

* in French: "Le point d'orgue": a pause over a rest which suspends the note value, the length of which can be prolonged at will.

timing – all these are errors, just as over-activity when calm is called for and retreat into silence when it is time to speak.

I would add that although the ability to remember oneself is our birthright, it needs first to be discovered and thereafter cultivated.

Lacking such special work, it will wither away. It is necessary, therefore – without exhausting oneself in fruitless efforts, but at the same time never giving up – quietly to try to develop this capacity by the frequency, duration and intensity of our attempts and by increasing their breadth and depth.

What does it mean to remember oneself?

I have been working at this practice for more than a quarter of a century and I have to admit that I feel as incapable now as I was at the beginning of describing it to my own complete satisfaction – I would say even more so than I was at first. For at the outset it seemed to me that I could clearly understand what it was all about. But I soon had to get rid of this lure. The attempts to remember myself soon swept away my cherished assumption that I understood, and I plunged each time into an even deeper abyss of incomprehension.

I was not alone in this predicament. Indeed the abyss was very densely populated! We were at sea, clinging to each other as we could. But our good Master, taking a malicious pleasure in keeping us there, and even in plunging us deeper, never failed, at the right time, to ask – with what perfidious wisdom! – the most innocent question in the world: "When you remember yourself, what exactly is it that you remember?"

Thunderbolt!

How could I know "exactly", except at brief moments, that I have to tear myself away from the perpetual dream of myself, except by intuitive hints of latent possibilities (sunken into oblivion, so to say), except by experiencing my lack of unity, coherence and any permanent or effective being? Except by default, if not finally by *reductio ad absurdum*?

But these are mere empty words. In this effort, all that can be known for certain is that I remember *nothing*. There is nothing that, without any possible doubt, I can call myself. Am I, then, *nothing*?

And yet, there is further evidence that cannot be denied. It is this – that whether or not it be active in me, the power is given to me to become aware, at certain moments, of my own presence: *I, here, now*.

This, when I experience it, is accompanied by a strangely familiar taste, a particular sensation that might be called "genuinely" subjective. It is, quite simply, I. I recognise myself. I remember myself. I.

Inevitably, this inner presence disappears. I lose it and I forget it. Then I find it again. I remember it – or, to be more accurate, it recalls itself to me.

"To awake. To die. To be born."

This saying, so dear to Gurdjieff . . . I am reminded of it, in this dilemma: on one side the recognition of my impotence and nothingness, on the other the certainty of this ever renewed power of being.

Faced with such a stumbling-block, such an enigma, I am tempted, like so many others, to abandon the game rather than argue endlessly or fall back on compromise.

But if I perservere – deliberately – by accepting to face it again and again; if I oblige myself to deepen my insight into the paradoxes of my inner situation, there may await me, at the end of this long tunnel, a very different prospect; a vision, and a new question – or the old question, yet transformed.

I remember myself.

Who is this "I"? Who is "myself"?

Who?

Let us think of a rider on his horse, cantering along the side of the mountain. "I" is the rider, "myself" the horse; "I" this individual essence, this potential being, "myself" this power of functional manifestation.

But the vision fades all too quickly.

My horse, because of his faulty education and the mass of influences to which he has been subjected – and both of these aggravated by neglect – has become a monster of egoism. He has been badly broken in, obviously – for, lo and behold, if he is not at this very moment perching on the shoulders of his rider and crushing him under his weight! Indeed, deprived of my mount, "I" am no longer a rider – not even a pedestrian, for "I", by myself, cannot move.

Once again, I remember myself. Once again, order is established and the vision reappears. Now the "I" no longer dreams, for the rider is once more in the saddle. With his hand securely on the rein, his mount will have no chance of straying down the path that leads to the precipice. Wide awake, the rider keeps an eye on "myself", the horse, and guides him unfalteringly along the ridge. The one keeping watch, the other carrying the watcher, they make a complete whole. Thus related, they will go far.

And yet, the question remains. "I", "Myself", a single being – but "Who" is this being? Who am I?

This "Who am I?", I was bound to find it again. Without my

knowing, it has never ceased to resound in the secret depths of my being. To know and to experience what I am, so that I may become it more truly.

To be able to grapple with the evidence one needs to be very simple. To the question "Who?" there can only ever be an echo – "Me". But this "Me" is unfathomable. This is precisely what is so difficult for us to accept – so prompt are we at reducing to the known what was on the verge of an opening onto immensity.

It is true, nevertheless, that this question of "Me" passes understanding and it is fair to say that my head, quite legitimately, finds itself unable immediately to grasp this fact. It wants to go on searching. Its role, after all, is to deal with ideas, to elaborate the picture I have of myself which needs to be sufficiently stable and self-affirming to stand up to the host of impressions that constantly assail it.

Does this mean, then, that nothing of a better quality is available to the mind? If it surrenders to something that it realises is beyond its scope, is there no other course open to it than to deny and suppress itself?

No. The mind is not the enemy, but rather the victim of the use I make of it. A reversal of this situation – a possibility that is always open – would enable the mind, in close relation with the other supports of human experience, to become the indispensable auxiliary in a general liberation from which the mind itself would benefit.

This reversal of the situation is the starting point in the process we call "remembering oneself".

Such an experience can be more or less fugitive and superficial. I can glimpse in it the evidence of a radical transformation which, if it develops, will affect not only the world of my thought but my whole being.

Yes, that is it: a new way of being. My attention is no longer the same, its power increases, its subtlety and its freedom both enlarge and enliven it. It mobilises in me latent forces that have hitherto been inert. This attention brings about a change in the capacity and rhythm of certain functions, thus releasing a series of processes by which the global perception I have of myself is intensified, a perception that is far beyond my ordinary level of sensation, the taste of which is quite unmistakable.

This general upheaval coincides with the emergence of a very intense feeling of renewal, a feeling of opening towards and belonging to the world without as well as to the world within, as though, in me, the two were one.

I am now permeated with certainty. What I have just experienced breaks through the narrow confines of my automatism, thus bringing me to obey a category of laws which, at my ordinary level of existence, cannot make themselves felt. From now on, supported by this experience, I cease to thrust aside as suspect the desire to study seriously those processes of transformation of energy which the great traditions have set before us as nothing less than cosmic laws.

Henceforward, I am activated, not by mere idle curiosity, but by the legitimate existence of a vision ampler and more accurate than before, of the possibilities open to me; and a wider understanding of the universal principles of relativity and analogy on which rests my hope of inner growth and liberation.

Thus we may say that at each level of existence the manifold components of our being are subjected to implacable laws. For the sleep-walker who spends his life as a "zombie", as well as for the impenitent dreamer who surrenders himself to the mirages created by an erratic imagination, the action of these laws spells perpetual enslavement. But he who awakens to himself can recapture, by dint of study and practice, the sense of an inner order as well as find the secret of the way in which his own energy is redistributed and regulated. Henceforth, he may hope to manifest himself increasingly in accordance with his true nature.

And so, what does it mean – to remember myself?

It is up to each one of us to hearken to the question without expecting any answer, to carry it within himself – yes, and to live it.

In the course of the evening some time had been arranged to enable members of the audience to put their questions.

Q. – One of your remarks in your lecture disturbed me greatly. You said, – if I understood correctly – that the role of a Master was not to bring someone to full awakening once and for all, but that it had to be attempted time and time again throughout the whole of one's lifetime. I thought that the Master – as in Zen Buddhism for instance – could at a certain moment wake a disciple up totally, but Gurdjieff did not appear to proceed in that way, if I have understood properly?

H.T. – The role of the master in the different traditions includes multiple aspects, and perhaps we indeed need not exclude this perspective of final liberation. Your reference to Zen Buddhism leaves me perplexed, because I wonder whether *satori* is synonymous, even exceptionally, with total liberation – I mean total and permanent. It seems that, in most cases, there is a moment of enlightenment which, like a flash *out of time*, could be interpreted as total liberation. But since man's existence is submitted to temporal laws, it could easily happen that he finds himself, just like Parsifal whom we mentioned earlier on, deprived of the Master's presence, deprived of the presence of that which had been able to transform him for a moment, and therefore compelled to find again *for himself* this possibility of contact with a higher reality.

Moreover it is true that Gurdjieff insisted on the necessity of a search that never ends. One of the aspects of his teaching is precisely the awakening of man to his destiny of seeker.

Gurdjieff wanted us to become "seekers of truth". If sometimes a lucky find or a happy encounter comes his way, they are immediately put into question, and again man moves forward, because he is not meant to become a statue of the Buddha but instead to be alive "within his life" thereby ceaselessly putting to the test the flash of understanding that he may have received.

Q. – Could one say that search, in the way Gurdjieff meant it, is akin to the Socratic idea of being "a midwife to men's thoughts"? In other words, could it be called maieutics?

H.T. – One may indeed wonder whether we could have here a kind of resurgence of the Socratic school and also whether in the Gurdjieff approach, we are dealing with something that is similar to that "helping give birth", which maieutics signifies. And no doubt we could find good reasons for not opening a rift between the teaching that Gurdjieff gave us and the one that pertains to this sage of ancient Greece. However, we don't know what Socrates' school really was. His Ouspensky was called Plato, but the latter made out of the teachings of Socrates by and large, a philosophy. And Gurdjieff was no philosopher. He even went as far as saying that philosophy was a form of drifting off course. Gurdjieff feared that real search might be transformed into empty speculation likely to induce the loss of the taste for more essential self-questioning.

Q. – Is the master himself permanently awake or only temporarily so? And does he come to awakening unaided or as a result of a teaching that he has received?

H.T. – I do not think that even in the very exceptional case of a highly spiritual man such as Ramana Maharshi was, could we interpret it as a spontaneous phenomenon. A Master does not arise on Earth without a past, without heredity. Nor does he arise just anywhere on our planet. He appears in a place which corresponds to the conditions of his conception. And a Master may have received all the conditions which predisposed him to be permanently awake, and yet prove himself incapable of reaching that level of realisation where a ceaseless renewal of his effort was no longer necessary.

What matters to someone who seeks truth, is to find a practical support for his quest; for this he would not require a man who is permanently awake. Very much the contrary, we can consider that the man who has never stopped searching, and who will go on searching till he dies, is a much stronger support for those who surround him than if he were to float very much over and above them, without being able to communicate his experience.

Q. – I believe that an awakened man such as Ramakrishna certainly was spent his time searching, according to what he said, and that he was very happy to be on the earth in order to search, even though he was permanently awake. Surely there must be some kind of situation which reconciles this total wakefulness and this quest?

H.T. – There certainly is a possible reconciliation, but here again, we would have to know who could be a judge of this? Can someone who is not on Ramakrishna's level know what was taking place in the inmost depths of his search?

However, if we interpret your thoughts slightly differently, more relatively, some measure of reconciliation would not be impossible. But whatever level of realisation a man may reach, might it not be necessary for him to understand, if he is a true Master, that this realisation cannot be completed, until he has accepted "to return to earth", until he, in his turn, has tried to wake up, with the appropriate means, those who are, like him, potentially able to find liberation?

Q. – How is it possible for someone who is conditioned to gain access, through his search, to something which is not conditioned?

H.T. – This is not possible, I think, if we look at your question from that angle. Man *is* totally conditioned. Even the privacy of his thoughts and his feelings is conditioned. Man is not free. If, from his conditioned state, he had, say, to jump over his knees, if he had to reach this threshold beyond which what we call the unconditioned is to be found, without any other means but those he has for ordinary existence, indeed there would be *no chance whatsoever* for him to do so. It remains to be seen, however, whether this so called "unconditioned" we long for, might not have some sort of corresponding echo in this conditioned being, whose existence is known to us, and if this is the case, there is no question of having to jump over our knees, but much rather of trying to track down what prevents us from being more really what we are.

Q. – Wouldn't this, then, be the negative way: I am not this, I am not that, etc . . . like a way of divesting oneself?

H.T. – Of course, in any kind of ascesis, there is always an element of apophatism. This apophatism which addresses itself to God, addresses itself equally to man. If there is a correspondence between man and God, it stands to reason that, for a time, a man refuses to consider himself reduced to or even totally identified with aspects of his external manifestations. He must be prepared, beyond all his denials of himself, to find something that, without words, is beyond any definition, any verbalisation.

Q. – Is it true that Gurdjieff said before he died: "I am leaving you in a fine mess", and how, do you think, should we understand this statement?

H.T. – (Repeating the question): "Gurdjieff is alleged to have said to his pupils before he died: I am leaving you in a fine mess.". It is true, but he didn't say it . . .

Q. – Could you say briefly how you yourself have moved on from the time you met Gurdjieff, had contact with him and followed his teaching? (laughter . . .)

H.T. – I must admit I would be quite incapable of answering this . . . especially in a few words! I think that those who knew Gurdjieff cannot but feel that a whole lifetime is not long enough to digest all that they received. All I can tell you is that the process is in progress. What was received as a living proposition at the time is *not less alive*, but *very much more alive* today than formerly.

Whenever I am directly connected with the memories of a particular event in my relationship with Gurdjieff, I feel immediately much closer in my understanding of him now than I did at the time. Without doubt, this must be a sign of a secret growth – not decay – of what he sowed in us.

Q. – (Pierre Schaeffer) It is not the answers that you give us which are bothering me, but the questions that are being asked. If I understood you well, you began by outlining a profile of Gurdjieff the man, and then you said that such a profile was not that important compared with his function. Those categories of the function and the man do not appear to have made much impact.

I wish to bring my own contribution by saying that, in reality, one does not assess that easily the problem of Gurdjieff the man, nor the problem of misunderstandings and the conspiracy of silence.

It is important to state that in lieu of only example and conformity to a model, he offered *dialogue*, and the means of this dialogue were new. Because dialogue, in general, is ineffectual. People speak, answer, don't listen to one another and reply to each other without actually saying anything. Here we had a new situation. It consisted of a certain number of rather bizarre pre-conditions, meant to shock, out of which came an exchange of questions. In this way any master could be replaced by anybody, in as far as he teaches the means of a dialogue, and to a certain extent anybody could become the master of anybody else.

H.T. – I like this insistence on the necessity of dialogue, this virtue of dialogue, if one compares it to certain clichés or images that one expects – rather too much – from the master. Where I am not totally in agreement with you, is when you speak of "anybody". In fact I would agree with you only in the case of a man, or some men, having the necessary quality to profit from this "anybody" – it all hinges on that. I think that if Lao Tsu or Confucius had met this "anybody" – and they did – they learnt from this "anybody". They would have been able to profit from a dialogue with him, and perhaps this is just what Socrates himself did. He was able to profit from just anybody in order to deepen his understanding and knowledge. However, I don't think that this applies to most of us, and I think that at least for a time – and I really do mean for a time – the master fills an indispensable function.

Pierre Schaeffer – I am not against what you say. "Anybody" for me is an ellipsis. It is the cliché of Master with a big M that I wish to try to destroy. I mean that instead of always emphasising Gurdjieff, his person and personality, I would not consider myself an unworthy disciple in saying that those who have received whatever it is from Gurdjieff, can, to the extent that they have learnt to practice such a dialogue, function as little masters just like anybody . . .

H.T. – There is a constant in the relation between master and disciple and this relationship can be found on different levels, and even perhaps at levels that one could consider as very inferior. However, I believe that there is a factor which one has to take into consideration, which is that the matter of knowledge is not uniform. It comprises differences of quality and between these different levels of quality, there are points of rupture. It is most probable that below a certain level, the relationship master-to-disciple, in its constant, would appear as derisory and ineffectual.

Nevertheless I follow your thought – if I am not mistaken – when you speak of a sort of relationship. There is, in whatever remains from the influence of a master on a man, his disciple, something which cannot entirely disappear and which is liable to come to life again, so to speak, with the help of dialogue.

L.D. – In what way does a right attitude towards Mr Gurdjieff clarify itself? What should the attitude of the pupil be?

H.T. – Never to forget what one is seeking from him. Never to lose sight of the fact that he is the master, but also that he is a man. And to keep a tight rein on any subjective reaction with regard to him. To be always on the *qui vive*. Not to let oneself be caught in the traps he sets. To know how to open oneself to him without surrendering oneself. To know how to exact from him the Word.

Interview

Q. – "Mr Gurdjieff", people often say. Is that, in your view, the most suitable way to designate George Ivanovitch Gurdjieff?

H.T. – I feel a little embarrassed to answer your question. I can only say that it is Mr Gurdjieff himself who invited us to speak of him thus.

Q. – May I ask why?

H.T. – We are here in the domain of hypothesis, because he was not prodigal with explanations! But he was obviously anxious to sustain in us a natural sense of respect, which went against the liberties taken nowadays with anybody who has something to *say*, and with whom one feels one has the right to talk endlessly – this was not quite the case . . .

However, let us not forget: there was his way of doing things, the manner of his approach, the complicity of a playful look, which would make up for the peremptory tone of the call to order, when he flung at one of us: "You not dog's tail! You pupil of Mr Gurdjieff!"

Q. – So we will say "Mr Gurdjieff". Now, Mr Gurdjieff spoke, if I am not mistaken, of *the work*; his disciples speak of *the work* and to my ears it is a bit like talking of "the Great Work" and it is, in any case "a huge affair". What is this work? And, first of all, what is its aim?

H.T. – The "Great Work" . . . yes . . . *There* is something to dream about! But I have the impression that there is a big risk of sinking into a sort of fantasy if one begins by defining once and for all the "aim" of the work, whereas what we learned to know as *work*, according to what Mr Gurdjieff meant by that, is above all an *experience*. Without doubt there was in us a more or less conscious motive at the beginning. But to be honest, it was only in the course of experience that we were able sometimes to approach, to sense, the real aim of this work, and first and foremost the essential need to which it responded: the need to awaken. To wake up from the state of confusion and torpor; from, in a word, the *ever-present sleep* in which we are immersed most of the time. To awaken to this power of presence

Interview with Robert Amadou for the magazine Question de, No. 50, Nov.-Dec. 1982, devoted to G.I. Gurdjieff.

which lives forgotten, buried in the depths, but which the work is naturally destined to rediscover, restore and cultivate.

Q. – You have written – surely following Mr Gurdjieff – surely following the Gurdjieff – that the aim of the work is "to remember oneself." Is the formulation authentic?

H.T. – Absolutely authentic.

Q. – You have also said and written, in a transcription of a conference at the Musée de l'Homme 15 years ago: "To remember oneself. What is it? God forbid that I should hold forth about it!" Is it only a rhetorical formula when you say that, or are the words to be taken literally?

H.T. – Between the two – or why not both?

Q. – And yet, you forbid yourself, you wish that Heaven should forbid you to talk about it. Why not talk about it?

H.T. – It is extremely dangerous. If we talk in the usual way resorting to analysis and comments, we risk losing contact with the essential. It is very easy to go adrift.

Q. – Mr Gurdjieff, however, speaks of a system and I remember reading a talk by him about a set of laws which were not easy, owing to their abstract nature and which seemed to me, if I may say so, to have a philosophical texture – speaking personally, I mean that as a compliment – and a very compact and solid philosophical texture. Isn't this, in part at least, the nature of the discussion?

H.T. – In a sense, yes. But it is the utterance of the Master: not words but *the* Word. And it is in my nature to distrust anything that claims to speak endlessly about a doctrine which has already been expounded as it should be.

Q. – So although you distrust a discussion on the Master's dissertation, you don't deny the right to the use of reasoning and intelligence, an attitude which is all too often to be found in so-called spiritual people. Thank you!

Another formula (I think it also is authentic): "The harmonious development of man". I will come back to this word "harmonious". But first of all, what is man?

H.T. – I wish I knew! But without going too far, I would say that man is a particular form of existence and this form has the privilege to reflect other forms whose meaning is much higher and much larger. But far from claiming to give a complete answer, I would rather hint that man is above all a question for man himself.

Q. – These other forms of which you speak, which are superior to man, do they constitute a hierarchy higher than man?

H.T. – Certainly.

Q. – Don't you think that Mr Gurdjieff judged it useful, necessary to distinguish between the psyche and the spiritual?

H.T. – Distinguish, yes, without any doubt. The psyche he refers to obviously belongs to the field of manifestation, whereas the spiritual belongs to what is real. But that does not mean a condemnation of manifestation in favour of essence. The prospect he opens is a prospect of achievement, through the fusion of the psyche and the spiritual, so that the manifestations of man emanate from his real essence instead of imposing themselves from the outside.

Q. – Is the "mind" (in the sense I think it was used by Mr Gurdjieff) into which psychic elements enter also a reflection of spiritual elements?

H.T. – It can be, but not always . . .

Q. – But to be able to be a reflection of the spiritual is its justification? The premise of its good use?

H.T. – Yes, of course. At the outset, the mind is not at all a distortion, an anomaly, a curse. It is instead an equipment which enables man to return to his real meaning. What remains to be seen, of course, is the use he makes of it.

Q. – What is death?

H.T. – A great mystery! . . . We are led to acknowledge in a human being the disappearance of a number of existential manifestations but is that the sign of a final death?

Q. – It amounts to saying that death is the passage to another state?

H.T. – It can be. For in other ways, it is sometimes given to us, in the course of our existence, to experience forms of partial death which free us and open us to another form of life.

Q. – Would you accept to apply to the system of which we speak a scheme common to all paths of initiation? That is to say the passage from darkness to light, from death to life; death allowing us to pass from a life which, as you were saying, was asleep, to a life which is an awakening. Is it in this way that the system belongs to the very general category of the paths of initiation?

H.T. – Nothing is more clear. It is, besides, confirmed in "*From the Author*" in the *Tales of Beelzebub*, when he quotes this phrase: "Without death, no resurrection" and reminds us that "all the prophets sent from on High and Jesus Christ himself have spoken of the death which can occur here, now, in this life that is to say the death of the "tyrant" which enslaves us all, and whose destruction alone can ensure the first great liberation of man".

Q. – What then is specific to the system?

H.T. – I feel like turning the question round. If I try to put the accent on the opposites and contradictions which exist between the different ways, I risk to lose myself; instead, my conviction grows of a natural (as well as "transcendent") unity of all the ways which inevitably take diverse forms, according to the external conditions which they encounter, and the objective requirements of adjustment which impose themselves.

Q. – In what does the teaching of Mr Gurdjieff differ from others as regards form?

H.T. – It is intended for the man of today. Far from being dissociated from the unique message transmitted, in their diversity, by the great spiritual ways, it attempts to define, in the present context, that which would allow our contemporaries to find again a true resonance.

Q. – How does this adaption to contemporary man reveal itself in the form of the system and its method?

H.T. – Initially, it rests upon a conviction that there is a misunderstanding and that we are inclined to confuse the fundamental ideas of the great traditional paths with the distorted images of them, projected by ordinary discursive thought.

Q. – Would that mean that the way opened by Mr Gurdjieff must at first be cleared of the obstacle of discursive thought before the seeker can engage in the way, which is analogous to other ways of initiation? And that therefore there will be a liberation or at least a better use of discursive thought than there was previously?

H.T. – Perhaps it is necessary to return here to one of the fundamental ideas on which the teaching rests: to understand that man is a "three-brained" being, in other words endowed with three brains, respectively granted intellectual, emotional and instinctive-motor capacities. He added, of course, that between thought, feelings and manifestations of the body, there should be simultaneity, convergence and reciprocal support, without which there is bound to be an imbalance and a drifting towards something excessive and distorted in one way or another.

Q. – The means intended to attain the aim, that is to say awakening, these means I am tempted to label techniques. Does this word bother you?

H.T. – Why not . . . ?

Q. – Do you then prefer "the method"?

H.T. – It doesn't matter which you use.

Q. – Mr Gurdjieff himself said "method", "technique", "path"?

H.T. – He used all of them, very freely.

Q. – This technique, this method, would it speak to the different parts of the human being?

H.T. – From the outset, it does so.

Q. – What is the principle of the method?

H.T. – It is the awakening to a reality, usually hidden, acknowledged as being endowed with a latent, potential presence, in spite of our difficulty in perceiving it and even more in making it manifest.

Q. – How does one proceed?

H.T. – I said there is a key to putting this teaching into practice. We have called it "self-remembering". If we set ourselves to define once and for all this idea, we can only betray it. Self-remembering has an aspect which is nearly inexpressible because it is too secretly, too intimately experienced by each one to be able to talk about it, hold forth about as we were saying earlier on.

Q. – What is, in the work, as taught by Mr Gurdjieff, the place and possibly the form of certain techniques that are found almost universally on the way of initiation? For example, the repetition of words, the litany . . .

H.T. – Ouspensky refers in *Fragments of an Unknown Teaching* to what Mr Gurdjieff called (concerning prayer) the "schools of repetition", inherited from ancient Egypt and on which the Orthodox liturgy is based. It is a door opening onto the knowledge of "what must be done" and of "how to do it", the very basis of the rituals inseparable from the great traditional paths. And yet, in his eyes, repetition if misunderstood carries very grave dangers, such as the risk of mechanisation, of stupid imitation, or of being lost in an indefinitely maintained sterile dream.

Q. – But doesn't the repetition which can be associated with breathing exercises have its uses?

H.T. – Undoubtedly, but under supervision. There is, besides, another aspect of this teaching which bears witness to that: the "movements".

Q. – Dance, well the movements that can become dance, that are perfected in dance?

H.T. – Yes, that's right! It is exactly through a return to an insistence on certain postures, that another understanding can open.

Q. – And of course, through the music?

H.T. – And through the music.

Q. – How do you explain the effect of these repetitions, of these breathing exercises, of these "movements" or dances in relation to the constitution of man you were speaking about earlier?

H.T. – Perhaps we should speak here of the learning of craft techniques or even more simply of swimming: it is not on the bank that one learns to swim, it is in full stream, as one is doing it. And that is just how the essential reveals itself to us, en route, at the very heart of the experience. The emphasis is always put on experience. Experience: what I pass through. What I go through and what goes through me.

In the course of practice, tranformations take place in me and I become aware of them, integrate them. The experience is centred on a meaning more real, more profound. It is then that a transformation of another nature takes place in me.

Q. – How do these processes work? Do they work at the same time on a physiological and a psychological level, for a spiritualization?

H.T. – Man remains whole – even in the disorder and the ignorance, he remains one. But if he wakes up and consciously takes part in the process, then the different components of his being, physiological and psychological if you wish, reconnect for a time. Magic – while it lasts.

Q. – But how are these practices particularly adapted? What is their analogy with man and the process of mankind?

H.T. – It is certainly not left to chance: it is meant to conform to laws. It is a matter of processes based on a real, objective science, where doctrine and method become as one.

Q. – We spoke earlier of "discussion", of a "system", of "mind". It seems now clear that the work allows for studies and the study of the doctrine, of the teaching. There is indeed a theoretical study which is part of the work. Is there also a place not only for practical exercises, but for meditation?

H.T. – Yes. Meditation. But what do we understand by that? The maintenance of an inner attitude, of an opening, of an availability; and this maintenance itself implies active participation with always the danger of being taken over again by a disconnected mind. But it is essentially, naturally, an invitation to the different parts forming the being to take an active part in the meditation.

Q. – "Harmony". The Institute that Mr Gurdjieff founded was called "The Institute for the *Harmonic* Development of Man". What is the difference between harmonic and harmonious?

H.T. – It is a question that I have often put to myself. But as for the answer. . .

Q. – Did you put it to Mr Gurdjieff?

H.T. – I did not have the opportunity to ask him this question. I was satisfied with my own resonance, of a natural association with music . . . The notion of "harmonic" evokes in me the objective evidence of a real correspondence. How not to refer here to the subtle resonances of certain Mongolian and Tibetan chants? But as soon as there is the least discord between mind, body and feelings, the "harmonic" cannot make itself heard.

Q. – We also spoke of the work, using only this word. Is there another word which can suitably help us to designate this science, this doctrine, this teaching and this method? I do not believe you would call it "Gurdjieffism"?

H.T. – Certainly not.

Q. – What would you call it or not call it?

H.T. – Certainly not "Gurdjieffism". Certainly not something which would put the accent on a doctrine not experienced, certainly not on a practice devoid of theoretical basis. Once again, the accent is put on experience. It is an experience which needs to be as global as possible.

Q. – Could one word sum up this globality?

H.T. – I would be *very* wary of that . . . I would be quite tempted to speak of the Gurdjieffian experience, if necessary, but I don't find that at all satisfactory either.

Q. – "Gurdjieffian experience" and not "Gurdjieffism" but it was, after all Mr Gurdjieff who taught the work, theory as well as practice. What sort of authority do you and the disciples of Mr Gurdjieff attach to Mr Gurdjieff?

H.T. – For those who approached him, it was immediately evident. It was enough to be in his presence – of course provided one was ready for it – to experience at once this presence itself as a source of understanding, as a fire capable of reanimating in us an independent power of perception and as an exigence full of understanding and benevolence. I repeat, it was in the nature of the evidence, and not deduced from any ordinary sequence of logical reasoning. In other respects I will go so far as to say that the influence directly received by us has lasted. If one of us strives in all sincerity to convey his own understanding, as he experienced it in Mr Gurdjieff's presence, what he is conveying is just a channel through which his influence can still circulate.

Q. – The irony of Mr Gurdjieff, his behaviour, with regard to alcohol and food, sex and money have often been considered as a provocation, and I believe you yourself haven't rejected this: provocation in the usual meaning, but also in the exact sense of the word which means call. His attitude provoked certain personal criticisms of Mr Gurdjieff. Could you say something about this didactic value of provocation?

H.T. – At the outset there is what became, through him, more and more true for us, this evidence of man's sleep. A sleep which can take many forms and which is sometimes very deceptive. Between sleep and dreams there are an infinite number of intermediate states which keep man on the fringe of his right and proper presence. Hence the necessity, sometimes, to intervene almost brutally to interrupt the course of these incontrollable wanderings, by the flagrant provocation of a behaviour which cannot fail to surprise.

Q. – More than a surprise, was it not a shock in many cases?

H.T. – A shock, yes. In truth a series of shocks.

Q. – I hope you will not find my question impertinent but I sometimes wonder if this provocation from Mr Gurdjieff was completely conscious, and I will explain why: some of Mr Gurdjieff's traits are shocking for everybody, and there are others which shock only those who don't know the Orient or Oriental people. It seems to me (and more than seems) that there were in Mr Gurdjieff, many Oriental characteristics that are moreover common in one way or another to Jews, Christians and Muslims (for example regarding money) which in themselves can be shocking to Westerners. Did Mr Gurdjieff make a deliberate use of the Oriental sides of his personality?

H.T. – I see what you mean, nor can I completely dismiss the idea. I think that he played on certain "Oriental" characteristics, and that he was aware of the provocation this represented for many of us. But maybe it was not so systematic. After all, he was as he was, and he did not calculate at each moment what his behaviour would be in an hour's time. He manifested simply as he felt was necessary at the very moment, while remaining aware of the effects which that might have on his entourage, and seeking in addition how to make the most of the change in the situation, in order to remain faithful to his vocation as a "spoilsport" – a hinderer of sleep.

Q. – What is, roughly at least, the part of biography, of history, in *Meetings with Remarkable Men*, and what is the part of fiction in it? Or is the question of no interest?

H.T. – We could maybe use a third word. Because it is certainly beyond these two aspects that something has to be found. He did not burden himself with historical truth, but equally he made use of all he had actually experienced – maybe each time in a different way: we heard from him quite discordant versions of how he had lived here and there, in the East or elsewhere. He remained absolutely free to contradict himself. But here again, what prevailed for him, was the present moment (the here and now). It was entrancing to see how he observed our respective reactions. It was not a cynical look, nor even ironic. It was a look of real interest and behind it (always there), the real wish to help each of us to awaken and to remain present to our own, proper reality.

Q. – Many readers must know *Meetings with Remarkable Men* from the film adapted by Peter Brook. Do you find this film faithful to the thought of Mr Gurdjieff?

H.T. – I have not the slightest doubt about the faithfulness of the filmmakers' intention: nor the least doubt about the difficulties that this must have represented, considering the demands of the film industry, as well as the limited resources involved – which perhaps explains and legitimizes in a way, certain forms of condensation in the making of the film which seem to be in conflict with what is evoked in the readers of the book.

Q. – Is the picture of Mr Gurdjieff and of the work which is suggested by this film to an audience ignorant of both, in general correct? I say "in general" and I am speaking of a suggested image.

H.T. – I think the suggestion remains faithful throughout, right up to the last frame of the film which bears witness, by the astonishing quality of the expression in the eyes of the young Gurdjieff, to his unwavering intention to pursue a search punctuated by a variety of experiences, none of which represented an end in itself.

Q. – What was, for Mr Gurdjieff, the part of tradition, of teachings he had received, and what the part of invention, that is of personal experimentation?

H.T. – I will turn that round: the Gurdjieffian inventiveness seems to me to be deeply traditional!

Q. – That does not exclude the fact that he may have received a teaching?

H.T. – No, he himself said that he received teachings, that he went and drew from different sources. And these teachings have lived on through him.

Q. – A reproach arises: that of syncretism; I am not the first one to use the word, I merely repeat it because one meets it here and there.

H.T. – There is certainly a basis for this concern, but that is precisely part of the experience: he was perfectly aware of the risk and of the obstacle which this represented for a number of those who came to him. He was sometimes snowed under with questions; but he made use of this very thing to affirm something which, over and beyond differences, was a much more direct expression of the experience he himself was living, nourished as he had been by diverse traditional teachings.

Q. – Is this use of various traditions applicable to the method as well?

H.T. – Yes, one can say that there is not any specificity which can be linked to a particular tradition.

Q. – And he added to it, you agree, a portion of invention? (I do not give any pejorative sense to the word "invention").

H.T. – No, to be precise, its true meaning – to discover – should perhaps be restored to it.

Q. – Yes, I was thinking in fact of invention, not in traditions exposed externally, but invention in itself.

H.T. – Yes, because his invention was much more of the order of a coming back to the evidence in a form which corresponded to a need directly felt . . .

Q. – Finally, it is the man himself who is attacked together with the teaching, when some go so far as to speak of luciferism or even of satanism, admittedly with ill intention. What are, according to you, the characteristics of Mr Gurdjieff or of his teaching which have served as pretexts for this kind of accusation?

H.T. – Certainly, there is a flagrant intention to provoke in the choice of Beelzebub as the source for understanding man's place in the universe. But one would be extremely naïve, it must be said, to let oneself be trapped in a narrow prison of ready-made ideas, because of the choice of a name; if one tries to read the *Tales of Beelzebub to His Grandson* without prejudice, I don't think that there is the least satanism or luciferism to be found in the words of Beelzebub: his submission to the Creator is much more convincing than anything that could serve as a basis for this accusation.

Q. – Did you see Mr Gurdjieff at prayer?

H.T. – Of course one must be in agreement about what one means by prayer . . . Yes, I can bear witness to that. I saw him pray – silently pray . . . Meditate. In meditation he was working with us, and, since meditation contains silence, we can testify that we shared silence with him, that we meditated in silence with him and that his presence was constantly perceived by us as a source of intimate conviction and of a more real conformity to what he was offering us. It was like a fundamental chord which sounded through the "melodic" developments of our respective sensibilities.

Q. – It is as easy to be mistaken about the word "prayer" as the word "God", and then prayer and God can mean everything and nothing. So I will be precise: What part does the grace of God play in the work?

H.T. – The largest, the greatest. Even if it is not said, even if it is not always acknowledged this remains nonetheless obvious.

Q. – On several occasions, when asked if it was true that Mr Gurdjieff, shortly before his death, said to his disciples:" I am leaving you in a fine mess", I've heard you reply that he did not say it, but it was nevertheless true. What does this paradox mean?

H.T. – I could tell you that it was obvious to us that we were in a fine mess, but it was *our* mess and not his. And his disappearance, in actual fact, made our real situation clear. We were much more able, thanks to all he had brought us, to acknowledge our position: we were now left to ourselves, so to speak, and it was up to us to take our destiny in our hands. But we were helped to take it in charge by all he had brought us before he left us, and his leaving itself was a sort of summons: "Now, it is your turn: from now on it is no longer my role."

Q. – It is possible to practice the work when Mr Gurdjieff is no longer physically present: this did happen and does happen to a certain number of men and women since his death. But is it possible to learn this work and to put it into practice efficiently by oneself? I mean just with the books of the teaching left by Mr Gurdjieff?

H.T. – Let us say that it seems if not impossible, at least improbable . . . Reading invites me to ask questions, opens perspectives, reveals the existence of a way and can arouse a legitimate interest in trying to reach a real knowledge of oneself. But however motivated they are, attempts shut in on themselves inevitably lead to new uncertainties, to new questions to which books seem to offer no satisfactory solution – *Fragments of an Unknown Teaching,* for example insists from the first chapters on the idea that *a man on his own cannot do anything,* on the necessity of working in a group and on the role of the Master.

Q. – To whom is the work addressed and how can one be admitted to the teachings given in these centres?

H.T. – To anyone who needs it – but truly needs it – and that is not "anyone"! . . . Mr Gurdjieff used to say that one must be "burning" from the sheer force of finding oneself faced with the most personal questions, the ones which hurt and which remain without answer, disregarding discouragement and holding in oneself the conviction that one is here for something: to find again the real meaning of one's own existence and to try to live in accord with it.

Q. – But admission to the work is subject to, if not an examination, at least the approval of those responsible?

H.T. – Yes, of course. No one has time to waste, have they? On both sides, moreover. If the candidate can open the wrong door – and it is sometimes obvious that he has – the responsible, for his part, is

certainly not safe either from making mistakes positively or
negatively! To engage truly, one must get to know each other: a period
of mutual probation is necessary before actual integration into a group.

Q. – Are dogmas and religious rituals an obstacle to the work,
from which the work would end up turning one away? Or are they
without importance for the disciple of Mr Gurdjieff, or else can he still
link them to the work?

H.T. – I will not say that they are without importance. I will first
insist that, at the outset there is no incompatibility. There will be
perhaps, in some cases, a questioning of the real value of belonging to
a religious way: is it a matter of an unconscious form of submission,
capable of being an obstacle to awakening or, quite the contrary, of a
privileged stimulus which helps the acknowledgement of one's own
lacks and of one's own betrayals at the same time as one's own
aspirations to real life? It is therefore a field of experience which is by
no means to be neglected, or refused, any more than to be arbitrarily
imposed. Thus, there is room among us for so-called atheists, as there
is room for believers of various faiths.

Q. – Do you know any disciples of Mr Gurdjieff who are faithful
churchgoers or in general of a religious persuasion?

H.T. – Yes, of course.

Q. – Does the work imply respect for a moral code?

H.T. – Certainly not, if you mean by this term a blind conformity
to a code of behaviour considered as "moral", and moreover very
often contradictory and which Beelzebub calls "chameleonlike". This
is a form of slavery from which it is urgent to free oneself: to believe
nothing at second hand and to rely only on direct experience, in order
to awaken to the innate exigence of a genuine *moral conscience*.

Q. – What, in your opinion, is the importance here and now of Mr
Gurdjieff's message and of the practice of the work carried out when
he was alive and which now continues?

H.T. – I am convinced that the teaching of Mr Gurdjieff can serve
as a ground for a more legitimate consideration of the big problems of
our time. He did not give us any particular indications on this subject
but it is up to us to do it: there is no prevailing doctrine in our groups
regarding the attitude to adopt towards the important social and
political problems.

Q. – At the end of an English book, *Gurdjieff Remembered*, by Fritz
Peters who had known Gurdjieff in his childhood, and then met him
again as an adult I read this sentence which touches me and will
surprise many readers: – "What I knew as a child, I begin to
understand as an adult: Gurdjieff practised love in a manner

unknown to nearly all men, without limit."

H.T. – It is a sentence which greatly touched me, because it is just that which stands out, when all is said and done, from the experience lived at Mr Gurdjieff's side, if one is not trapped by this or that anecdotal memory. Unbounded love, neither left to chance nor without a price: a love of extreme exactingness, born of this suffering at seeing us prisoners of our numerous misunderstandings, and attempting by all possible means to evoke in us the feeling of urgency, the thirst for return, for union, for communion with the essential.